C000000343

# Why Your Boss is Programmed to be a Dictator

## A book for anyone who has a boss or is a boss

## Chetan Dhruve

First published in 2007 by:

Marshall Cavendish Limited
119 Wardour Street
London W1F 0UW
United Kingdom
T: +44 (0)20 7565 6000
F: +44 (0)20 7734 6221
E: sales@marshallcavendish.co.uk
Online bookstore: *www.marshallcavendish.co.uk*

and

Cyan Communications Limited
119 Wardour Street
London W1F 0UW
United Kingdom
T: +44 (0)20 7565 6120
E: sales@cyanbooks.com
*www.cyanbooks.com*

A CIP record for this book is available from the British Library

ISBN-13 978-0-462-09902-6
ISBN-10 0-462-09902-4

Designed and typeset by Curran Publishing Services, Norwich, UK

Printed and bound in Great Britain by
TJ International Ltd, Padstow, Cornwall

For my parents
Vinodchandra and Damayanti Dhruve

and

Diana Eden
Some teachers don't just teach; they change lives.

# CONTENTS

# PREFACE

Badly behaved bosses and a workplace characterized by nervousness and fear are inevitabilities. Or so we have come to believe. A workplace where people are encouraged to challenge, where bosses listen, where information is given openly and freely, and where people are treated with respect is not too commonplace. Have you ever wondered how it is that people who are strong and confident outside work become compliant and unquestioning when they are at work? It is a question worth examining. That is what Chetan does in *Why Your Boss is Programmed to be a Dictator*. He provides explanations that are not commonly acknowledged but when you think about them are obvious. And their consequences are ones that anyone who has ever worked in an organization will doubtless recognize. Consequences that are often unpleasant and occasionally downright shocking.

The majority of management books look at organizations as a collection of individuals. They focus on individuals' behavior. Most training courses do this too. They tackle leadership and management skills as if they can be separated from the context in which they are applied. The fact is, they cannot. The environment in which the managers operate is a strong, often unacknowledged force that determines how people behave when they are inside any given system. In this book Chetan shows that the environment is an all-powerful influence – for good or ill, and that few are able to "resist" succumbing to the pressures that the environment brings to bear.

This book is a breakthrough. Using fascinating and relevant case studies Chetan shows how easily even the least likely person can become a dictator-like boss, usually causing a great deal of fear, stress, inefficiency, and, in extreme cases, fatalities. For managers who have been struggling to create more innovative, inspiring, and successful workplaces these pages will reveal answers that have so far been scant in the business section of the bookshop.

Sally Bibb
Series Editor

# ACKNOWLEDGMENTS

Writing a book is one thing. Getting it published – every writer's dream – is quite another. As all first-time unknown authors know, getting the word out in print isn't easy. It takes not just hard work, but a series of events to make things happen. And it takes some very special people to make those things happen.

So here's a heartfelt thank you to those special people – Shaun Orpen, Sally Bibb, and Martin Liu. Without these critical links in the chain, this book would still be "a good idea" running around in my head, driving me crazy. In particular, I'm indebted to Sally for her kindness, understanding, help, and encouragement – shown to a virtual stranger halfway across the world. If ever there's a Milk of Human Kindness award, Sally deserves it.

Writing is usually considered a supremely solitary activity, and so it is. But a book is essentially a team game, a bit like cricket – though players perform and score individually, it's the team that ultimately counts. In turning my manuscript into the polished product it is, I'd like to thank the team: Martin and Pom of Cyan, and Sarah Lockwood of Curran Publishing Services.

A big thank you to my sisters Uma and Nina for being an invaluable part of my education. If it wasn't for their consistent urging when I was in school, I'd never have read a book; I'd still be devouring comics. A special thank you to my wife, Sonali, for taking the journey with me.

Thank you to Padma Venkatraman, friend and fellow writer, for her confidence in this book. Thanks also to family and friends who have willingly helped with this project in one way or another – Sharbani Augustine, Kalamanda Cariapa, Maya Culas, Vijay and Rita Dhruve, Praveen Paul, and Ramesh Sivaram.

Most of all, I owe an apology to my four-year-old son, Arjun. His regular entreaties of "Play cricket with me, dad" were usually met with "later," "not now," or any other manner of parental brush-offs, so much so that he's stopped asking me to play altogether. If the cricket world has lost a budding Brian Lara (Arjun bats left-handed), the fault is entirely mine.

Nearly all men can stand adversity, but if you want to test a man's character, give him power.

Abraham Lincoln

# PRELUDE

■ On a foggy Sunday afternoon in March 1977, a jumbo jet carrying holidaying retirees was taxiing along the runway of an airport on a Spanish island. As he peered out through the cockpit's windscreen, the plane's captain suddenly noticed some lights eerily heading straight towards him. Before he could get out of the way, the lights smashed into his plane. The lights were those of another passenger jumbo jet. The result was the worst aviation accident in history, which left 583 people dead.

■ Nearly ten years later, in 1986, a space shuttle blasted off from its launch pad in Florida on a freezing January morning. Just 73 seconds after lift-off, as a TV audience of millions later saw, the shuttle disintegrated. All seven astronauts on board were killed.

■ In February 2003, a space shuttle entered the earth's atmosphere after completing its mission. The spacecraft streaked high across the California coast, flying at 23 times the speed of sound at a height of 231,000 feet. The shuttle headed home to Florida but a few minutes after crossing the coast, it broke apart over Texas. Everyone on board died.

■ In March the same year, the US President declared war on Iraq. He somberly addressed his people on television stating, "On my orders, coalition forces have begun striking selected targets of military importance to undermine Saddam Hussein's ability to wage war." The President's intelligence chief had earlier told him there was no doubt that the Iraqi dictator had weapons of mass destruction. After the Americans rolled into Baghdad, they found no such weapons.

Centuries after his death, what do Lincoln's words have to do with these seemingly disparate events?

# INTRODUCTION

## Why another book on bosses?

Imagine you're ill. You visit your doctor. He prescribes a course of treatment that requires you to go to the hospital the next morning.

"Don't eat anything before you arrive," he says.

You normally have a large breakfast. On the morning of your hospital visit, you feel even hungrier than usual because you're conscious of the doctor's instruction. You spot a pizza slice in the fridge. You think, "Only one slice. I'm sure the doctor won't mind."

You eat the pizza slice and go to the hospital. A nurse gives you some medication. You start throwing up. The nurse gives you some other medication to stop the retching.

Let's start again with the same situation. As before, the doctor says, "Don't eat anything before you arrive."

"Why?" you ask.

"Because the medication we'll be giving you when you arrive will make you want to throw up."

It's morning again. You eye the pizza slice in the fridge. What are you going to do? You're going to obey the doctor's instructions.

Generally, there are two kinds of books on bosses. The first kind teaches you, "Here's how to survive a bad boss." The second

1

kind teaches you, "Here's how to be a good boss." Of course, the latter books talk about managers and management or leaders and leadership – these words being sexy names for bosses and bossing. (Imagine a book title: *One Minute Bosser* – won't go down well, will it?)

If a doctor gave you instructions and didn't tell you why, wouldn't you ask? But the existing books don't seek to ask why. They're like the nurse who will help you with the symptoms. While it's obviously useful to have relief for symptoms, it's even more important that we know the cause of those symptoms.

Why don't existing books address the cause? They don't because they assume they already know the cause: "bad" or "wrong" behavior. These books assume that bosses are in control of their behavior and that you are in control of your behavior – because only if our behaviors are under our control can we change them. These books mistake the symptoms for the cause. Hence they say, "Do this. Do that. Don't do this. Don't do that." So let me first tell you what I won't be talking about.

## What this book is not about

This book will not ask you to change your behavior so you can better handle your boss. If you're a boss, it will not ask you to change your behavior so you can be a better boss. Hence I stress, here are the kinds of things this book is not about:

- how to deal with a bad boss
- how to manage "upwards"
- how to impress your superiors so they make you a boss
- how to be a terrific leader
- the 50 laws of leadership
- ten skills all leaders must have
- 25 ways to outwit an evil boss.

Now having told you what this book is *not* about, let me tell you what it is about.

## What this book is about

When we have bad bosses, it's not just that we blame them, but we blame them with the fury of self-righteous indignation. Of course he's at fault. Of course she's to blame. If only he was nicer, if only she had an iota of people skills, everything would be fine. All our anger is directed at the individual. It just seems so logical.

But rather than blaming bosses, this book asks the question, "Why do bosses behave the way they do?" As you know from your imaginary hospital visit, it's very important to have an answer to the question "Why?" That way, we can find a cure for the "disease" of bad bosses. If we find out what causes bosses to be bad, we won't have to spend our time, effort, and energy on the symptoms.

It's not that we haven't tried our hands at a few "cures" – we know employees should be more empowered, and bosses should be more humane. Concepts such as self-management or "servant leader" already exist. The problem is even though these concepts appeal to us, we still cling to the boss–subordinate top-down model. Why do we do this? We do this because we have a deeply entrenched belief that bosses are a necessary evil of working life. We believe there's no alternative. So we have beliefs, not a real "knowing" or understanding. How do we get from belief to knowledge? By asking the question "Why?" If we have an answer to that question, we will have a real reason to change.

In answering "Why?" this book makes the radical argument that we can't blame bosses, because they're not in control of their behavior. Not only is your boss not in control of his behavior, you're also not in control of your behavior. And your colleagues also aren't in control of their behaviors.

What do I mean by not in control? I certainly don't mean that we all run around like demented headless chickens. What I mean is that despite our individual differences, there are certain baseline behaviors at the office that are common to all of us. And there's something mysterious that's causing all of us to behave in a particular way.

These behaviors are entirely predictable, like the results of a software program. A program is simply a set of instructions a computer follows, with predictable results. Similarly, our behaviors at the workplace are so predictable that they may as well have been programmed into us. Make a person a boss, and you'll pretty much know in advance how he's going to behave.

What if we could find out what that mysterious program was, and change it? What if we could get your boss to change his behaviors, *without asking him to change*? Impossible? There's even more. The book will also investigate why you behave the way you do, and why your colleagues behave the way they do, and why the organization behaves the way it does. And how we can change all this without us having to undergo training to change.

All this may seem like a mighty task. But as is often the case with seemingly complicated things, once you get it down to a simple and easily understandable idea, everything else falls into place.

In taking this journey, we'll be traveling through many fields such as social science, engineering, medicine, psychology, and Darwin's theory of evolution. One more thing – as you know, there are three steps we need to take when we think something's wrong with a situation:

**Step 1**: Recognize and accept that something is indeed wrong. This admission is extremely important because otherwise, we will continue living in the make-believe world called denial.

**Step 2**: Once there's an admission that something's wrong, we need to find out what's wrong. We need to understand what's really going on.

**Step 3**: Once we understand what is wrong, we need to figure out how to change the situation.

This book spends most of its time on the first two steps. As with most problems, once you complete the first two steps, the third step becomes obvious. Having said that, although the third step is "obvious," this doesn't mean it's simple or easy. This book does not have a magic bullet that will wipe out all our problems. As such, this book's ambition is modest in that it offers a beginning, but no neat and beautifully wrapped-up ending. Ultimately, more than getting you to do things differently, my aim is to offer you a different way of looking at the world, so you realize why we need to do things differently.

## Why I wrote this book

I've had my fair share of bad bosses. I've worked for large companies and tiny startups, a public sector organization and private sector ones. I've worked for blue-chip companies and unknown ones. I've worked for male bosses and female ones. I've worked in a Western country and an Asian one. I've worked with people from a wide range of nationalities in a range of fields.

Despite all the variety, I found bosses were mostly the same. After going through several of them, I realized something strange was going on. The moment someone became my boss, there was an instant change in attitude and behavior. The change was subtle, yet paradoxically obvious. And it was happening far too regularly for the phenomenon to be something related purely to individuals. Otherwise normal human beings were immediately turning into proper bosses. This is not to say that I've only had bad bosses – there have been good ones and average ones too. But the bottom line is that bosses are bosses.

It wasn't just my bosses who would change. I would change too. The minute I got a boss, I was a different person with the boss, even if that change was not overt. So an otherwise "normal" person – me – was turning into a proper subordinate.

Whenever I had trouble with a boss, I blamed him or her for my misery. But I also blamed myself because when you have a bad boss, here's what most of the advice-givers say: "Don't blame your boss, look into yourself for the reasons." What that really means is, blame yourself first.

So I blamed myself for a long while but that wasn't making any sense either. Surprise, surprise, it turned out that I wasn't the only person in the world with bad boss problems. It seemed to be happening all over the place. But you had to look hard for it and notice the smallest of signals because no one talked about it openly. Almost everyone I asked admitted to having a bad boss – or several bad bosses – at some point in their careers. "Admitted" is the operative word, because it's not easy for people to admit to this.

It's disquieting to see what happens when you ask people about a bad boss, even a boss in the past. Their mood changes instantly and they anxiously wonder why you're asking. Sometimes they get defensive. Why are they becoming tense? The truth is, the trauma still has a hold over them. They fear that somehow, their future will be affected – even if they don't need a reference from the old boss or no longer work for him. But if you scratch the surface hard enough, a bad boss story comes tumbling out. And once it comes tumbling out there's no stopping it. This is because perhaps for the first time, the "victim" has got an opportunity to really talk about it.

I began wondering why this phenomenon was so prevalent. Seemingly nice people turned into monstrous bosses in an instant. Seemingly intelligent and assertive people turned into quivering wrecks in the presence of overweening and arrogant bosses. Seemingly pleasant colleagues turned into shameless backstabbers.

What was going on? Why were people behaving like this? This book is an attempt to answer those questions.

# Section

# I

## The Problem We Won't Talk About

# 1

# WELCOME TO THE
# MODERN OFFICE

## Jane's story

Jane's boss, Tom, asked her to come in for a meeting. When she went to see him, he barked, "What the hell do you think you're doing?"

Jane asked Tom what specifically he was talking about, but he continued screaming and questioned her competence. Jane was bewildered but wasn't given a chance to respond. After he finished his tirade, Tom curtly indicated the door to her. Jane's heart beat faster and her hands turned clammy as she left the room knowing her job was at stake, but without knowing why. She needed the job. She had a family to support. But she also knew her boss had no right to speak to her abusively, though she felt utterly incapable of fighting back.

The following week, Tom's boss, Bob, summoned her for a meeting. Bob began by saying, "As you know, we have been very unhappy with your performance. Your manager brought this to your notice in your meeting with him last week, but you have done nothing about it since then."

Jane started to reply but Bob cut her off. He simply said, in the manner of a king bestowing a gift on a wretched peasant: "We are giving you the opportunity to resign, rather than dismissing you."

Jane had no idea what had gone wrong. The only occasion she could think of when she had attracted her boss's ire – in the form of a glare – was when she informed him about a complaint a major customer had made. She wasn't associated with the project the customer had complained about. But the customer's representative was based in Jane's building and often had hallway conversations with her; he had asked her to express their dissatisfaction to her boss. The customer thought it would be better to complain informally first, before getting into contractual and legal issues.

Jane had thought her boss would appreciate the early warning, but evidently she was wrong. In retrospect, it hadn't been a good idea to have told him. It was too late though.

Jane sent her resignation to Tom and was invited by Sandra, in human resources, to attend an exit interview the following Friday. Jane accepted the invitation as she was itching to finally give her side of the story. But at the interview, Sandra looked distracted. It was 4.30 pm, and noticing that Sandra wasn't really paying any attention to her, Jane asked Sandra what her weekend plans were.

Sandra instantly brightened up and said that she was going away on a weekend holiday trip, and needed to leave soon. She asked Jane, "Do you really want to say anything? I need to go and anyway, why waste your breath on a company you're quitting?" Jane quickly said her goodbyes and left.

A few days later, Jane landed a job interview. She was asked, "So Jane, why did you leave your previous job?"

Jane knew the drill – she wasn't stupid. She wasn't going to blame her ex-boss. That would be suicide. If she blamed her ex-boss, she would be classified as a whiner and a person with authority problems.

Jane looked at the interviewer straight in the eye and lied, "I'm looking for newer and better challenges."

## Peter's story

Peter's boss, Marcus, had given him some very high-priority tasks, along with a low-priority task that required Peter to index some files. Peter had been working very long hours for a couple of weeks when one evening, Marcus asked him, "Have you finished the indexing yet?"

Peter replied, "No, because I've been very busy with the higher-priority work that you want done before we meet our customer."

Marcus, knowing fully well that Peter's workload was immense, asked, "What hours have you been working?"

Marcus was always in at 9 am and left at 5 pm. Peter said, "I'm in the office by 7 am, and I'm here until midnight."

"What have you been doing between midnight and 7 am then?" Marcus retorted angrily.

## Ruth's story

Ruth's boss, Julia, sat in a cubicle right next to hers. Every morning, Julia would give Ruth a long list of things to do, without discussing them. Julia would insist on emailing rather than talking about tasks or issues. She wanted all discussion to happen on email. In her emails, Julia often deliberately made ambiguous statements and left out relevant information. In case Ruth had any doubts, Julia would not give her clear replies.

Ruth would press on with her work as best as she could. But there were several times when she was unable to finish the work because of the information that Julia was deliberately withholding. Then without warning, Julia would suddenly pick out the unfinished tasks only in front of customers and yell, "Why didn't you do this?" Both Ruth and the customers would squirm with embarrassment. Since Ruth wouldn't want to confront her boss in front of their clients, she would stammer out an apology.

11

After a while, Ruth couldn't take it any more. She began looking for a new job.

## Stefan's story

Stefan and his team had successfully completed a long and difficult project. To celebrate this achievement, Stefan's boss, Trevor, announced there would be a celebration for the team at a pub nearby. Trevor often held work-related meetings at the pub after working hours.

Once the team had finished for the day, they headed to the pub with Trevor for their celebration. Everyone enjoyed the relaxed atmosphere. At around 7 pm, Stefan told his boss, "I need to leave. Bye everyone, see you tomorrow."

Stefan had a family consisting of his wife and two young children, and he wanted to get home before his kids went to bed. He also didn't like the extended drinking sessions that ended with predictable results.

As Stefan turned toward the pub's exit, Trevor called out sarcastically, "You're no team player."

## A story from the military

Every afternoon, a US army general would get drunk. He'd then order subordinates to salute his dog.[1]

All the stories you've just read are true stories, though names have been changed.

What's common to all these stories? Well, no prizes for guessing: a bad boss. All of us have had our share of terrible bosses. If by some quirk of fate you haven't had an awful boss yet, I have the sad duty of giving you some unpleasant news: you're going to be lumbered with a beastly boss at some point in your career. And there's nothing you can do about it. In the meantime, count yourself exceptionally lucky for your good boss, go down on your knees, and give thanks.

But for those of us who daily live through the hell that is a bad boss, here's the killer: we cannot and will not talk about it openly. You never know what goes on between the closed doors of a boss–subordinate relationship. Often, like abused children or spouses, subordinates are too ashamed to admit what's really going on. It's like a shameful secret.

# 2

# THE WORLD'S WORST KEPT SECRET

At work, what are you not supposed to talk about, above all else? When you're interviewing for a new job, what are you not supposed to talk about, above all else? Although your human resources people may ask you, what must you not talk about, above all else? And especially with your boss, even if asked by your boss, what must you absolutely, absolutely not talk about, above all else?

You know the answer, but you won't talk about it because you've been trained not to. The answer is: a bad boss. You cannot and will not complain openly about your boss. You'd rather just resign. You're not alone. As the saying goes, people leave bosses, not companies. Bad bosses are a fact of life. Yet you're not supposed to talk about it. When I asked the subordinates whose stories you just read if I could use their real names, all of them said no.

When was the last time you went up to someone at the office and said, "Hey, I've got a bad boss"? Have you ever attended a company-sponsored training course titled "How to deal with a bad boss"? Although there are many books on bad bosses, would you bring one into your cubicle and leave it out in the open for everyone to see?

No, because even the person who's climbed to the very top of the US corporate ladder advises us to not complain about our bosses. In his book *Winning*, Jack Welch, retired CEO of the corporate giant GE, devotes an entire chapter to "That Damn Boss." To his great credit, Welch acknowledges that bad bosses exist. But he warns against complaining about your boss because it's going to backfire on you: "There is a reason why kids don't tattle on bullies. Unfortunately, the same principle applies in the office."[2]

Given the reality of today's workplace, Welch's advice is obviously well-intended. But it only goes to show how deeply entrenched and widely accepted this notion is. It's as though it's a law of physics – an immutable reality of life. So a whole industry has been built around helping you cope.

There are books, websites, support groups, companies, and consultants. You get told about the various species of bosses that inhabit our workplaces: we have the manipulators, jerks, dictators, bullies, pacifists, or consensus-builders. We have the details-oriented nit-picker or the big-picture visionary. We have the hands-off manager versus the hands-on manager versus the manager who's never there. We have the alphabet soup of Type A personalities, Type B personalities, or Type Z personalities. We have the control freaks, the paranoid, the narcissists, the neurotics, and the psychotics. Then we have the animals: lone wolves, cuddly bears, alpha males, and mothering females. The list is endless and a remedy is prescribed based on the kind of person, personality type, or animal you're dealing with. Take your pick.

Choice is good, right? Think again. Finding out your boss's type can be confusing and takes a lot of work. Is he a bully boss or just a highly driven Type A alpha male? Is she a consensus builder or a mothering hen? Once you figure out what type of boss you have, you need to base your behavior around that. This is not easy, as you know only too well. Nonetheless, you do all the hard work and figure out your boss is a "lone wolf" and behave accordingly.

Unfortunately after only six months, there's an organizational change and you get a new boss. All your hard work has gone down the drain and you have to start all over again. Worse, what if you get it all wrong? What if you think your boss is a consensus builder, when in fact he's a lone wolf? What if she's an alpha woman hidden beneath the demeanor of a mothering female? There goes your "Outstanding" rating, along with the long-sought promotion, increment, bonus, and new-big-house-in-a-posh-neighborhood plans.

On top of those who offer to help you deal with bosses, there are experts who try to help the organization on a grander scale. There are re-engineering pundits, change-agent chameleons, management consultants and of course, leadership gurus. But their well-meaning efforts are often wasted. The consultants are thrilled when they see you enthusiastically jump up and down on their training courses, only to be deeply disappointed when you and your colleagues lapse into old behaviors barely a couple of weeks after the training.

Why don't you listen to these people? Why aren't you putting their carefully thought out instructions and sincere entreaties to good use? Why won't you change? No one will tell you, but the reason you stick with your current behavior is simple: it works! You're not stupid. You still have your job. You are a survivor. Consultants come and go. You are the one who has to deal with your boss. And you know your boss better than the consultant knows your boss. No wonder you continue to do what works.

"Keep going and don't complain about your boss" is the modern version of the story of the emperor's new clothes. For those unfamiliar with this insightful story by the 19th century Danish writer, Hans Christian Andersen, let me recount it. Even if you do know the story please read it again, because you've probably only heard the part about the emperor not wearing any clothes. There are subtleties in the story that are often missed out.

## The emperor's new clothes

Many years ago, there was an emperor who was besotted with clothes and high fashion. One day, a couple of con men came to him and introduced themselves as gifted tailors. They told the emperor they could make a wonderful new suit for him – a suit from a new type of cloth that was extremely fine and light. That wasn't all, the suit also had an amazing quality: it would be completely invisible to anyone who was stupid, incompetent, or unfit for his office.

The emperor thought it was an excellent idea to own such a suit because, beyond making him look good, it would help him identify the non-performers in his administration. He duly agreed to the con men's offer.

But the "tailors" had no plans of making anything. They pretended to work for several days and when the "suit" was "ready," they invited the emperor to take a look. Although the emperor was eager to see his new suit, he was a little nervous. He wondered that if he couldn't see the suit, it would mean he was unfit to be emperor. So he asked a minister to first check out the suit.

When the minister entered the room, he couldn't see the suit. He stared and stared, but saw nothing. Noticing this, the cheats asked the minister if he didn't like the suit. Knowing that he would be dismissed from his job if he told the truth, the minister told the con men that the suit was indeed splendid, with delightful colors and designs. He went out of the room and reproduced this report to the emperor.

Then the emperor himself entered the room and also saw nothing. But since he couldn't admit to being unfit to rule, he too declared that the suit was amazing. All the courtiers were invited to see the suit and all of them proclaimed that the suit was indeed magnificent. The con men were highly praised and rewarded for their efforts.

Word spread about this fantastic new fabric and the subjects now clamored to see the new suit. A minister requested the emperor to undertake a procession to display his new clothes to the public, and the emperor gave his assent.

On the day of the procession, the emperor undressed. Then, assisted by the con men, he put on his new, non-existent suit. As the procession began, the people cried, "Look at the beautiful new clothes our emperor wears!" No one wanted to say the emperor was wearing nothing, for it would be an admission of stupidity.

This went on for a while until a child yelled, "But he's not got any clothes on!" Soon, everyone was whispering the same thing. The emperor knew his subjects were right. But having invested so much dignity in the suit, he carried on even more proudly, with his courtiers carrying the invisible train following him.

In modern parlance, the child was a "whistleblower" – someone who shouted out the truth. As you go through the rest of this book, keep in mind these three things about the story:

- No one wanted to speak out the truth.
- Even intelligent and powerful people kept quiet.
- After the child yelled out the truth, the emperor kept going as though he was still right, despite knowing the truth himself and knowing that everyone else knew the truth.

If you're tempted to laugh condescendingly at this story as a relic of history, hold on, because we've got our own modern version of this old tale.

## The modern emperor

If our president or prime minister ran out on the street without any clothes on, we'd probably literally blow whistles – and we'd all start laughing at him immediately and continue laughing about the incident for decades to come. The episode would be replayed over and over on TV and spread far and wide via the Internet.

We may laugh at our leaders, but we also have our own modern emperor who we dare not laugh at: the boss. The boss is the biggest emperor's new clothes story of our time. What is it about us, apparently free people, that we will not speak the truth about our bosses? Like the emperor's intelligent and powerful ministers, why do intelligent and powerful subordinates keep their mouths shut?

There are two reasons. The first one is obvious – it's going to backfire. Like the emperor's subjects, we're worried we'll metaphorically lose our heads – our jobs. In her excellent book *The Stone Age Company*, Sally Bibb gives the example of a friend of hers, a person she greatly respects. Her friend got a new boss, a much younger person who was throwing his weight around. Sally's friend told her that he was scared of his new boss.

Sally says, "I was amazed at this. How could such a capable and successful manager be scared of this chap who seemed like he didn't even deserve much respect? It was simple. He has the power to fire my friend if he gets on the wrong side of him or doesn't play the game, so my friend is allowing himself to be held hostage to this man. Don't get me wrong, I can understand why. He has a family to support and bills to pay. He has been in the company a long time, and feels that he doesn't have many options. [H]e knows that unless he plays the game in the way his new boss wants it to be played, he will be out."[3]

Here lies the crux of the matter. People are scared of their bosses primarily because they know that if they don't toe the boss's line, they are going to be axed. It's not just the jobs they lose; it's the whole package – the money, health insurance, self-respect, image in the community, kids' education, plans for the future, and so on. There's a huge amount at stake.

So these are not trivial fears. They are visceral, gut-wrenching, sleepless-night-giving, heart-beating-faster fears. Although a job-loss doesn't result in physical death, it's scary enough. Of course, people can always quit and do something else. It's not the end of the world to lose your job. The underlying fear is this: what if you get a bad boss again?

The second reason we don't "tattle" on our bosses is that complaining about your boss makes you a victim. In today's offices, complaining is the defining act of victimhood. Implicit in victimhood is a lack of toughness. And because being tough is so prized, not only do very few people complain about their bosses, the ones who do are seen as weaklings unable to take on the rigors of working life.

The inevitable result is that bad bosses continue to thrive. Bad bosses are a big, big problem. Organizations suffer because productivity nosedives and good people leave. Individuals suffer because bad bosses inflict tremendous stress – ranging from petty harassment or mild emotional abuse to sexual harassment or outright physical assault. Because of bad bosses, careers are destroyed and lives are ruined. People change jobs, move out of town, go to court, or even quit working. Even worse, some people kill themselves.

You know it, I know it, everybody knows it. So let's admit to it: bad bosses exist. They don't just exist, they infest virtually every office at one time or another, everywhere in the world.

Yes, there are some exceptionally good bosses. But why are bad bosses so common and why has nothing been done about it? Well actually, something is already being done: training, training, and more training. Lots of it.

Far more crucially, we've done something apparently path-breaking. We've gotten rid of the word "boss" and its variations such as manager or supervisor, and replaced these words with a much nicer word: "leader." Of course, there are those who say leaders lead and managers manage. Nonetheless, if you have people reporting to you, you're considered a leader.

What are we trying to do by calling people leaders? We think we're doing two things. First, we are being accurate – since managers lead teams of people, they're obviously leaders. Second, if we call people leaders, we hope they will behave like leaders are supposed to.

It's often said that those who don't know history are condemned to repeat it. We're not the first ones to try changing words in a bid to change reality. To see how, let's go back in time a few hundred years ago to a city called New Amsterdam.

# 3

# BOSS:
# A BRIEF
# HISTORY

In the 17th century, settlers from Holland arrived in a place called New Amsterdam. With them they brought the word "baas," a word that slaves used to address their masters. The word was used in South Africa too, where the Dutch also settled.

Although they were in New Amsterdam, the Dutch weren't in their native country but in the United Sates. New York was New Amsterdam in those days. Over time, the apparently impertinent New Yorkers corrupted baas to boss.

Today, we don't call people master. Neither do we address them as boss. Job titles such as team leader, manager or supervisor disguise the inbuilt hierarchy inherent in the word "boss." And typically, we call bosses by their first names.

Are you fooled by this apparent freedom and lack of servility? No way. If you want to find out someone's boss, just look at the kind of language you use:

- Who do you report to?
- Who's your manager?
- Who manages you?

■ What's your reporting chain?
■ Who's your superior?

Implicit in each of these questions is the assumption that some-one has power over you. More than anything else, what defines the modern workplace is power. Even if your workplace is one of these super-flat super-modern organizations where everyone is called "associate," do you ask a colleague "Who's your asso-ciate?" Oh no. You ask, "Who's your boss?" You cut through the vague verbiage and get straight to the point.

In short, what are you really asking? You're asking, "Who's your master at the office?" You probably think that's stretching things a bit. No one owns you at the office. No one can physi-cally whip you if you do something wrong. Unlike slaves, you don't come under laws that govern property and chattel.

So yes, this is stretching things a bit. But let's consider some-thing that's common to all people, slaves or non-slaves: feelings. There are people who wake up with their hearts racing and sweat pouring out of their bodies because they have to go to work and face the boss. Some cry daily in anticipation of their descent into hell. As they approach the office building, they're overwhelmed by a sense of dread.

While subordinates may not get physically beaten, millions of people are routinely emotionally whipped by their bosses. Unlike physical injuries, which tend to heal fairly quickly, the emotional scars can linger for years, perhaps decades. People suffer from depression, anxiety, and other psychological distur-bances from the trauma this causes. Not for nothing has the term "wage slave" been invented.

In contrast, if you have an exceptionally good boss, why do you feel so happy at your good fortune? Why the joy? Why the relief at being so lucky? It's because you know how blessed you are. There's no doubting that slaves felt the same way: if they got a good master, they considered themselves tremendously lucky.

The point is, while we definitely don't suffer the extreme conditions that slaves did, we still experience those emotions to a great extent. Why? Because there are similarities between our conditions. There's a similarity between baas and boss. Modern comforts and technology may surround us in our offices, but what's going on inside us is often a different story altogether.

To see how the boss–subordinate relationship continued to be such a top-down one, let's fast forward from the 17th century to the early 20th century. In 1911, an "efficiency expert" named Frederick Winslow Taylor wrote a highly influential paper called "The principles of scientific management."[4] The paper went on to become a huge hit in those days, especially with the likes of Henry Ford, who asked Taylor to help make his car-making assembly lines more efficient.

In his paper, Taylor talked about a management style for those workers who were "mentally sluggish" and therefore weren't suited to doing any thinking. Under this style of management, here's how the workers were supposed to behave: "When this man [the supervisor] tells you to walk, you walk; when he tells you to sit down, you sit down, and you don't talk back at him."

Obviously, this was the command-and-control method at its micro-managing best. Taylor himself stated that this method was "rough" and not suited to intelligent laborers. But he said that management needed to do this so that "mentally sluggish" workers could perform their tasks with maximum efficiency.

We're a long way from those days, because organizations are less rigidly hierarchical than they used to be. We have far more freedom than workers did in earlier times. People are better educated. But we're still living with the remnants of Taylor's legacy. Bosses often assume their subordinates are "mentally sluggish" (ie, stupid), and hence feel the need to dictate. We still behave in a way such that when "this man" tells us to do something, we do it without questioning, because the consequences of questioning are not pleasant. In effect, we dumb ourselves down, or to use Taylor's terms, we present ourselves as mentally sluggish in a classic case of the law of unintended consequences.

Having said all this, we've made the transition from baas to boss and we live in a correspondingly fairer world. We're now trying to move to an even more equitable world. To do this, we're transitioning from boss – under its various guises such as manager or supervisor – to a vastly different word: leader.

Anyone who's in charge of people or has people reporting to him is called a leader. And then, to turn leaders into better leaders, they are put through leadership training courses. The question is: can you train someone to become a leader? Even if you have great leadership skills, does that make you a leader? Just because you lead people, does that make you a leader? The answer to all these questions is a resounding no.

Equally, you could think, "I don't need a book to tell me that my boss is a dictator." You have enough evidence for it already – your boss is abusive, always orders people about, doesn't tolerate dissent, and inspires fear. So, just because your boss does all these things, does that make him a dictator? No. What is the right answer then?

Why are we even getting into definitions here? We need to do this to understand why bosses behave the way they do. One of the beauties of language is that if used properly, it can throw up solutions to problems or at least tell us why a solution can't be found. You may think this is a storm in a teacup, a squabble over semantics. But as you'll soon see, the transition from boss to leader isn't as straightforward as it sounds.

# Section

# II

# Understanding
# the
# Problem

# 4

# THE HIDDEN FACTOR THAT INFLUENCES OUR BEHAVIOR

To find out what's going wrong in our organizations, we need to first figure out who a leader is. In the context of leading people, who is a leader? It's important to understand this because what's causing the problem is that we're not defining "leader" properly.

## So ... who is a leader?

There's already a vast amount of material out there dedicated to answering that very question. Most of the material, if not all of it, states that a leader is someone who has multiple abilities: the ability to inspire, motivate, serve, set visions, craft goals, communicate, delegate, praise, "lead from the front," empathize, sympathize, be emotionally intelligent, "walk with kings – nor lose the common touch," and so forth.

But these skills are the answer to a "What" question – "What skills should a leader have?" It's not an answer to the "Who" question – "Who is a leader?"

To understand this better, try another question: "Who is a wife?" Take a traditional answer: a wife is someone who's loving, gentle, kind, sweet, devoted, faithful, and say, a great cook. While this sounds right, it's actually the answer to the question, "What kind of person should a wife be?" The answer to "Who is a wife?" is quite simply, a woman who's married. Before you can be a good wife, you first need to be a wife.

Similarly the answer to the question "Who is a leader?" is profoundly simple: a leader is a person who's been elected to lead by the people he/she is leading. We have a different word for someone who assumes power and leads without being elected: dictator.

Allied to the words leader and dictator we have two other words: citizen and subject. Citizens are people with the power to choose their leader; subjects have no choice in who leads them.

Let me give you those definitions again, to emphasize how important they are:

*Leader:* A person who is elected by the people he or she is leading.
*Corollary:* A person who leads without being elected is a dictator.

*Citizen*: A person who has the power to choose the leader.
*Corollary*: A person powerless to choose the leader is a subject.

Remember: if you lead without being elected, you're a dictator.

In organizations today, the terms "leader" and "leadership" are casually and lazily tossed around, without any real thought being given to those words. But it's critically important to get the definitions right, because it's only then that we can work out what's going wrong and what needs to be set right. If you use the wrong words, you can set yourself up for failure since your expectations won't match reality.

If you labeled a donkey as a tiger and expected the donkey to behave like a tiger, would it? No. Would you consider the donkey a failed tiger? No. Would you try training the donkey to behave like a tiger? No. Anyone who even tried would be a fool.

Yet we do exactly the same thing at the office – we label people as leaders and expect leadership behavior from them. But what we get in real life is something else: boss behavior. To continue the tiger/donkey analogy, the problem will be compounded if the donkey looks like a tiger. We'd wonder why the tiger that we can see with our very own eyes is behaving like a donkey. Similarly, when we see a man in charge of a bunch of people, he sure looks like a leader. He's got people reporting to him. His people even call him their "team leader." But why then are we getting dictator-like behavior?

The reason is that there's a hidden factor that causes people to behave the way they do. To understand this, we need to find out what drives human behavior. When someone does something, what do we look for as a way of explaining his or her behavior? Usually, we talk about genes, family background, personality and so on. We assume that the person's behavior is a result of something unique to that person.

This is a reasonable assumption to make and it's an assumption we make often. But, and it is a very big but, is it a reasonable assumption? To find out, let's take a look some research and real-life instances, starting with a famous experiment that was conducted by social scientists at Stanford University in 1971.[5]

## The Stanford Prison Experiment

The lead scientist on the experiment, known as the Stanford Prison Experiment (SPE), was Philip Zimbardo. He said the purpose of the experiment was to find out, "What happens when you put good people in an evil place?"

Our normal and logical response would be that if the people were good, they would behave as good people do, and if they were evil, they would behave accordingly. But is this what would really happen? That's what the scientists wanted to know.

The scientists created a mock prison in the basement of the psychology department's building. The prison was made as realistic as possible, with steel barred cells, a closet which functioned as a lockup for solitary confinement, and an exercise yard.

The scientists then advertised for male volunteers. Of those who responded, the scientists selected only those who were psychologically and physically healthy. So this was a group of normal, middle-class young men. Randomly, half of these men were assigned to be prisoners, and the other half were assigned to be prison guards.

To simulate what real prisoners go through, the prisoners were then put through a series of dehumanizing experiences. They were "arrested," taken to a police station, fingerprinted, stripped, searched, doused with anti-lice spray, given prison uniforms to wear, and were referred to not by their names, but only their identification numbers. And onto every prisoner's right foot a heavy chain was bolted on.

For their role, the guards were given khaki uniforms, whistles, and dark glasses. They were told their job was to maintain order in the prison. To do this, they were allowed to do what they wanted, within certain boundaries.

Once the experiment started, what followed was astonishing. The guards took to their roles with great enthusiasm and began using their power over the prisoners. They stripped the prisoners, made them do push-ups, forced them to clean toilet bowls with their bare hands, and so on.

Christina Maslach, an assistant professor, recalled having a pleasant chat with a "charming, funny, smart" young man, waiting to begin his shift as a guard. She was told by other researchers that he in fact was particularly sadistic. When she viewed footage of him at "work," she said, "This man had been transformed. He was talking in a different accent, a Southern accent, which I hadn't recalled at all. He moved differently, and the way he talked was different, not just in the accent, but in the way he was interacting with the prisoners. It was like [seeing] Jekyll and Hyde. ... It really took my breath away."[6]

In retaliation, the prisoners rebelled by barricading themselves in their cells, taunting the guards and tearing off their identification numbers. As the experiment progressed, things got worse: the guards behaved increasingly more sadistically and the prisoners rioted. Some prisoners even had to be released because they were severely traumatized.

Zimbardo, the lead scientist, had taken on the role of prison superintendent. He found that he himself got sucked into the role, rather than being the objective scientist he was supposed to be. The experiment was scheduled to run for two weeks. But Zimbardo ended it after just six days because the experiment was no longer a simulation: it had become real.

Perhaps the most dramatic illustration of this was the change in the behavior of the top consultant to the SPE, who had taken on the role of the parole board's head. A former prisoner himself, he became so authoritarian that he "felt sick at who he had become – his own tormentor who had previously rejected his annual parole requests for 16 years when he was a prisoner."[7]

From the experiment, Zimbardo concluded that our behavior is much more under the control of external situations than we realize. Far from being under our command, our behavior can be governed by the circumstances that we find ourselves in.

Many have disputed not only the ethics of the SPE, but also its conclusions. However if we just look around, real life does seem to support the SPE's findings: two notorious examples being the events at Abu Ghraib in Iraq and Guantanamo Bay in Cuba.

Abu Ghraib was a prison under Iraq's dictator Saddam Hussein. Thousands of people are reported to have been tortured and executed there under his regime. Following the Iraq war and Saddam's ousting, US forces used the same prison to house those they had captured.

You almost certainly know what happened after that. You've probably even seen the ghastly pictures. The US soldiers who worked as prison guards began brutalizing and humiliating their prisoners. The guards:[8]

- Arranged naked male detainees in a pile and jumped on them.
- Tied down a prisoner and attached him to a leash held by a guard.
- Terrified prisoners by taking ferocious dogs very close to their faces.
- In a particularly infamous case, the guards hooded a prisoner, made him stand on a box and attached wires to his hands and private parts. They then told him that if he fell off the box he was standing on, he would be electrocuted.
- Took photographs of dead Iraqi detainees.

What made the US soldiers behave in such abominable fashion? After all, they were supposed to be different from Saddam's henchmen. The Americans were meant to be an example of how civilized people behave. They were Americans for heaven's sake – freedom loving, human-rights respecting, happiness pursuing, apple-pie eating, Statue of Liberty Americans.

Anticipating the hazards of being told to harden their stance, one US military intelligence officer had even counseled, "We need to take a deep breath and remember who we are. We are American soldiers, heirs of a long tradition of staying on the high ground. We need to stay there."[9] But in sharp contrast, rather than being the opposite of everything Saddam stood for, the guards could quite easily have been functionaries of Saddam's brutal gang.

Similar events have taken place at Guantanamo Bay, the US detention facility in Cuba. Prisoners have tried rebelling by going on hunger strikes, and some have even "succeeded" in killing themselves. Prison guards have been accused of torturing prisoners.[10]

In both cases, you would assume that beyond having US values, the Americans were better fed and better equipped than their prisoners. There was no "social injustice" reason for them to torment their prisoners. But this didn't stop them from behaving the way they did.

Zimbardo said of the Abu Ghraib abuses that although he

was shocked, he wasn't surprised: "What particularly bothered me was that the Pentagon blamed the whole thing on a 'few bad apples.' I knew from our experiment, if you put good apples into a bad situation, you'll get bad apples."[11]

It's not just Americans who behave this way of course. Prison authorities, the police, and military forces around the world are guilty of the same behavior when they have power over people. It's a very common phenomenon.

The veteran BBC journalist John Simpson has covered several murderous conflicts. In his book, *Strange Places, Questionable People*, he wrote about an incident in the war in ex-Yugoslavia. An elderly man lived in an old age home with several other old people. Most of their carers had fled. The seniors relied on the old man to chop firewood, to stave off the bitter cold. The old man was shot dead by a sniper nearby for no apparent reason. Simpson noted, "The longer I spent in Sarajevo, the more I decided that the proper distinction was not the kind of constitutional right and wrong. ... It was the difference between people who had power and people who didn't."[12]

It's relatively easy to understand this phenomenon because we've seen it over and over and over again. We even have sayings like, "Power went to his head" or "Power corrupts. Absolute power corrupts absolutely."

You may think that the power of power is unique in being able to change people's behaviors. So let's look at another experiment, milder than the SPE, to see what happens when people are put into a different kind of situation.


## The Good Samaritan experiment

You're probably familiar with the story of the Good Samaritan – a person who helped a distressed man lying on a road, when other religious folks just moved along without going to his assistance.

What prompts a person to help someone in need or ignore him? As before, our immediate answer would be that it depends on the person. If the person is fundamentally good or kind-hearted, he's very likely to help. If he's stonehearted, he's unlikely to do anything.

Scientists J. M. Darley and C. D. Batson conducted an experiment based around the story of the Good Samaritan.[13] Theology students – who we'd assume are kinder-hearted than your average Joe – were asked to give a talk in a different building. One group of students was told they had to hurry because they were already late; another group was told that they had just about enough time to get there, and the third group was told they had some time to spare.

A "victim" was placed on the path leading to the other building. He lay slumped on the ground and made moaning noises. How did the individual students respond? The answer is surprising. It's not a straightforward "helped" or "didn't help." The answer is, "It depends." It depends on the amount of time a student had.

In fact, some students were even told that they were to deliver a lecture on the parable of the Good Samaritan. It didn't matter; what really mattered was whether or not the students were in a hurry. If they had more than enough time, they were very likely to help and if they had no time to spare, they were unlikely to help. So the main thing that influenced the decision to help was how much of a hurry a student was in. Some students in a real rush even stepped over the victim in their bid to get to the next building on time.

Both the SPE and the Good Samaritan experiment indicate that people's behavior depends on the situation they find themselves in. But the Good Samaritan experiment and the SPE are only experiments. If it's true that a situation makes us behave in ways that depend on that situation, has anyone used this theory in real life? The answer is yes. Step forward New York City.

## New York City's crime wave

In the 1980s, New York suffered from a great deal of violent crime. The question was, how to bring it down? Conventional logic would argue that the police should concentrate on solving serious crime like murders or violent assaults. It didn't make sense to go after seemingly petty things like graffiti or drunken behavior. Moreover, conventional reasoning would also dictate that to prevent serious crime, we first need to address the root causes – issues such as poverty or unemployment.

In contrast to conventional logic, there's a theory called "broken windows" that argues just the opposite. The theory, formulated by professors James Wilson and George Kelling, says that if there's disorder, it's likely that more and more crime will be committed, increasing in the degree of seriousness too.[14] So if a window is broken in a building and not replaced, it sends out a signal that there's no order in the area, that no one is in charge, and that no one cares. A cascading effect begins such that other windows are also broken. Soon the whole area wears a dilapidated look. This sends out the message that in this place, anything goes. It doesn't matter if the windows are in a good or rundown neighborhood.

The theory is that if police pay attention to minor offences like graffiti, they can prevent serious crime from occurring. After Rudolph Giuliani was elected mayor of New York City in 1994, he turned conventional logic on its head. He brought in William Bratton to head the city's police department. Bratton was a fan of the broken windows theory, and told his police force to catch the people who were creating minor disturbances.[15] The cops began hauling in people for relatively trivial offences such as urinating in public, trashing streets, demanding cash after forcibly washing car windows, or covering walls with graffiti.

The idea was that the near zero-tolerance of petty crime would send out the message that somebody was actually in charge, that this was a place where order was maintained. The results were dramatic. Crime fell sharply, even when compared with other major cities in the country. According to Bratton and Kelling, the number of murders in the city fell from 2,262 in 1990 to 629 in 1998.[16]

There's some debate about whether it was broken windows that led to the decline in crime, or whether it was other factors that led to the drop – most controversially abortion.[17] There were also accusations that the police became too heavy-handed and infringed on people's civil rights.

Having said that, you can do a little "thought experiment" with broken windows yourself. Imagine you're walking on a filthy, litter-strewn street, and you have a piece of chewing gum in your mouth that you need to get rid of. Nobody is around. No one is going to notice or care if you spit out the gum.

Now imagine that you're walking down a really clean street, where there are trashcans at regular intervals and a fine is payable for littering. The people around you are well-dressed, and you spot a couple of cops nearby. In your mouth is the chewing gum that you need to spit out. Under which of the two situations are you more likely to spit out the gum? You may not even be consciously aware of the cleanliness of the street you're on, but whether or not you spit out the gum will depend on the situation.

The lesson from these experiments and real life experiences is that our behavior can be strongly governed by external circumstances that we may not be conscious of. In his brilliant book, *The Tipping Point*, Malcolm Gladwell calls this the Power of Context.[18]

Put another way, something outside of us can strongly influence how we behave, a factor that we're not usually conscious of. At our workplaces, what's that factor? It's a version of the Power of Context – the system. But what do I mean by the "system"?

# 5

# THE SYSTEM

The word "system" is used in many different ways for many different things – from road systems to computer systems to home theater systems. It's used for anything and everything. We even blame lots of things on "the system," as though it's an all-purpose, all-sucking black hole into which we can conveniently throw things away.

So what exactly is a system? I'm going to focus on one particular definition of the word.

> *System:* A system is an entity that maintains its exis-
> tence through the mutual interactions of its parts.[19]

Without the parts or the interaction, the system breaks down or ceases to exist. A system has an identity of its own that is greater than the sum of its parts. A great example of a system is the human body. If we remove the body's parts – the heart, lungs, kidneys, legs, and so on – and place them in a pile on the floor, the entity "body" no longer exists. The body's existence depends not only on the individual parts, but also the interactions between them.

A critical ingredient of a system is what's called "feedback." This is the process in which when a part acts, it provokes a response in the system. When the system responds, it in turn influences the parts.

Imagine you have trouble breathing. Your doctor diagnoses a lung problem and prescribes some medication aimed at your lungs. But after you take the first dose of the medicine, you develop a headache and your hands start tingling. You complain to your doctor, who informs you that the headache and hand tingling are well documented "side-effects." She tells you not to worry.

What are side-effects? These effects are feedback – they are responses from the body system. While the medication is treating your lungs, it's also affecting the whole body system. If your doctor didn't know any better, she'd examine your hands and head, to see what was wrong with those individual body parts. And because she wouldn't find anything wrong with those particular parts, she wouldn't know what was going on.

Another good example of a system is the weather, where you cannot examine things in isolation. You cannot determine local weather conditions without reference to what's happening globally. What happens in one part of the world affects the weather somewhere else.

To study systems, there's a field of study called "systems thinking."[20] In systems thinking, we try to understand things by looking at them as a whole and understanding the interactions between the parts.

This contrasts with traditional analysis, which examines things by taking them apart. We place a great deal of importance on analytical thinking. Analytical "problem solvers" are highly sought after. Here's what we typically do when we analyze a problem: we break it up into smaller and smaller bits, till we get to the smallest bits. We analyze each bit. We then try to figure out what's wrong with each bit, and fix each bit. We then expect that since all the bits are fixed, the overall problem will go away.

The analytical approach has its uses, of course. It works for straightforward problems or challenges, which is not to say these challenges are necessarily easy. The challenge could be difficult and complex, like sending a man to the moon. This project can be accomplished using a linear, analytical approach with a series of logical steps. Once a man goes to the moon and returns safely, the "problem" is "solved."

These solvable problems are called "tame problems," a term coined by a couple of professors: the late Horst Rittel and Melvin Webber at the University of California, Berkeley.[21] Tame problems are solvable in that you can clearly define the problem, gather information, and work towards a solution. Once there's a solution, that's where the problem ends.

The world isn't that simple a place, though. When things start getting complicated and there are various interdependent factors, you have what Rittel and Webber call "wicked problems." The analytical method falls flat when dealing with wicked problems. You can't simply use analysis because it's very difficult to do the bare minimum when tackling a wicked problem – you can't even clearly define the problem. Further, one thing impacts something else, which in turn impacts something else and so on, without end.

Wicked problems usually have characteristics such as:

- There's no definitive formulation of the problem.
    - Your answer depends on how you formulate the question.
- They don't have a definite ending.
    - There's no way of saying it's finally over.
- There are no right or wrong answers.
    - Instead, things could be "bad" or "good." Or things could "get better," "get worse," or simply "be satisfying." Further, these answers could vary depending on who is giving the answers.
- There's no ultimate test of a solution.
    - Every implemented solution will generate "waves" of consequences over time.
- There are several ways to explain a problem.
    - For example, crime can be explained by not enough police, lack of opportunity, weak laws, easy availability of guns, and so on.

Here are some examples of wicked problems:

- How do we stop terrorism? (Define terrorism, who started the fighting first, how far back in time should we go?)
- How do we wipe out poverty? (Is lack of education the real problem, how do we get people to be less corrupt, shouldn't we first stop the civil war?)
- How can we get countries to cooperate on world climate? (Some countries may not even agree that there's an environmental problem.)

To "solve" or better understand wicked problems, we can use systems thinking. Using this kind of thinking, we get answers that could be very different from those obtained by analytical thinking. For example, take a problem like traffic congestion in a big city. The analytical solution to the problem of heavy traffic is to build more roads. What actually happens when you build more roads?

London's ring road is called the M25 Orbital. It's the world's longest ring road and was meant to remove congestion from central London. The idea was to get people to drive around London rather than through it. In effect, the M25 was a "more roads" solution. What actually happened?

To understand this, we can use a systems "loop diagram" to show the relationship between roads and car usage of the M25.

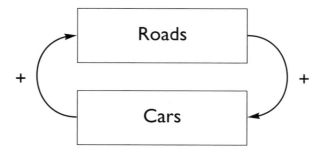

The plus signs indicate that both move in the same direction – "more cars" begets "more roads" and "more roads" begets "more cars."

More and more people started using the M25, so that the M25 itself was getting clogged. So the "more roads" solution led to more cars, a reinforcing loop. Because of the regularly immobile traffic, the M25 is often labeled as Europe's biggest car park. The answer to this congestion would seemingly be again, more roads – create additional lanes on the M25. But that would again aggravate the problem.

So to solve the congestion problem, we need a different approach. There's now talk of introducing a "congestion charge" to reduce traffic on the M25. Motorists will have to pay to use the road during peak traffic hours. A similar charge is already in force in central London, and has reduced congestion there by 40 percent during peak traffic hours.[22] In terms of a diagram, here's what it looks like:

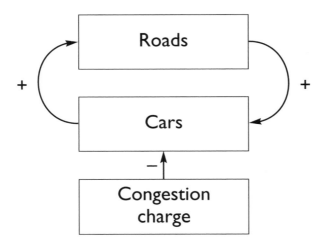

The minus sign near the up arrow (going from Congestion charge to Cars) shows they go in opposite directions – as the congestion charge goes up, the number of cars goes down, which reduces the congestion and the need to build more roads. As you can see, systems thinking can provide us with very different answers from analytical thinking.

Keeping all this in mind, let's get back to our offices. Typically, systems thinking is applied to things or processes. But let's apply it to something else: human beings and their relationships. What's the one thing that matters the most in an organization? As the cliché goes, it's about people. It's about the interactions between people – it's about wicked problems.

Usually, when we try to "solve" the behavior of individual people, we use the analytical approach: "He's poor at leadership. Give him leadership training." Or, "She doesn't say what she thinks. Give her assertiveness training." But when two people interact, that's a system. We even have a label for this system: "relationship." As long as there is an interaction, the relationship exists. If one person opts out, the entity "relationship" breaks down and ceases to exist. This holds true for all kinds of relationships – friendships, business associations, marriages, and so on.

Fundamentally, leadership arises from the interaction between two individuals: the leader and the individual being led. A leader cannot exist in isolation. But when talking of leadership, analytical thinking throws up a "leader" – hence the glut of material on the subject of leaders. But in reality, because there's an interaction between the leader and the led, we have a system. This means we should look at leadership not analytically, but through the approach of systems thinking.

## Leadership is a system

You can't have a leader if you don't have a citizen who has elected that leader. When a person votes for a leader, and the leader accepts, it's a form of interaction. This means what? *That leadership is a system.* The day the person withdraws his or her vote, votes for someone else, or the leader resigns, the interaction breaks down, as does the leadership system. Hence, it's wrong to talk of leadership as though it's the exclusive domain of leaders. When talking of leadership, we also need to include the "followers."

Let's look at this through an organization chart. If you're asked to draw a conventional org chart, here's what you would come up with:

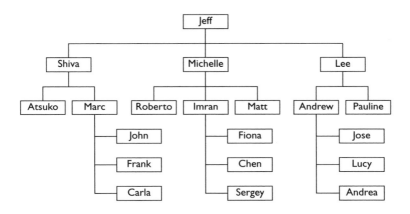

Before you drew this chart, did you stop to ask yourself, "What do I want to represent?" Not really. You drew an org chart that looks like the one above because that's what all org charts look like. In contrast, what is the first thing you normally do when you want to draw something? You ask, "What do I want to draw?" In the case of the above chart, you don't ask that question, but you draw a chart that has this answer – "The flow of power from the top to the bottom." The question to that answer is, "What's the flow of power in an organization?"

So what the org chart actually represents is this, though it's implicit:

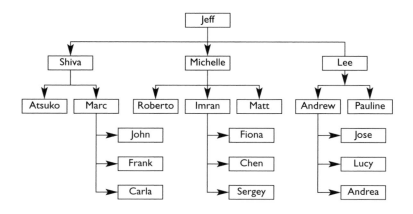

If we take a snapshot of the chart at any level, here's what we see:

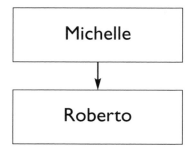

This snapshot represents only the top-down power flow, ie Michelle is Roberto's boss. It is linear thinking such that A impacts B – Michelle impacts Roberto.

But what should we really want an organization chart to represent? We need an organization chart to represent the things that make the organization work: its people and the interactions between them. Whenever we have interactions, we have a system; hence we need to draw a systems diagram to represent the interactions. In terms of interactions between two people, here's what the diagram would look like:

The downward arrow represents Michelle's behavior (that of a boss) and the upward arrow represents Roberto's behavior (that of a subordinate). So Michelle's "leadership" of Roberto is intertwined with him. It's the same for all boss–subordinate relationships – so here's our regular top-down chart again, but one that reflects the behaviors between bosses and subordinates.

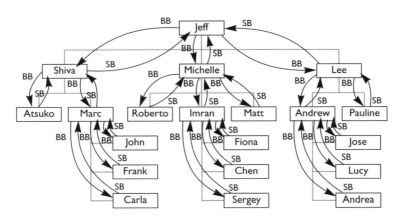

BB: boss behavior        SB: subordinate behavior

Looks quite messy, doesn't it? But it's more accurate in terms of showing us that the interactions between bosses and subordinates form systems. The fact that you cannot isolate the leader from his or her "follower" is central to the whole issue of leadership. Let's look at this with a couple of examples.

# 6

# A STORY OF
# TWO LEADERS

Take for instance Mahatma Gandhi. He was leader of India, a colossus across generations. But for now, forget about all his accomplishments and so forth. Go back in time to when Gandhi was alive, in the first half of the previous century. The British Empire had ruled India for a couple of hundred years. The Empire also had several parts of the world in its mighty grip.

Keep your nationality aside for a few minutes. If you were Indian at the time, here's your challenge: you want independence but you have to fight an infinitely stronger force. How do you do this?

First off, you'd need to get yourself a great leader to stir the masses out of their fatalism, defeatism, and apathy. After being lorded over for a couple of centuries, the people don't have much of a fight left, let alone arms and money. It would need an absolutely inspiring leader to get the country out of this morass of depression. And India isn't an easy, homogeneous country – people are divided along the lines of language, caste, ethnicity, and religion. This is a country not of millions but hundreds of millions. How do you go about finding such a leader?

Take the contemporary, conventional approach. We get ourselves the best headhunter there is. We appoint a panel of experts in leadership and begin our hunt for India's leader. We invite several candidates for our interview – Gandhi wasn't the only leader on offer to the Indian people. There were also several highly committed and motivated revolutionaries who thought Gandhi was a rosy-eyed, idealistic, head-in-the-clouds dreamer. Not a doer for sure.

You interview several revolutionaries. All of them are impressive speakers, have real zest for the cause, and are willing to die for it. They're full of energy and have even brought well-thought-out plans to defeat the enemy – attacking strategic targets and causing mayhem among the British troops. Despite their limited means, they already have an impressive track record of blowing up ammunition dumps and denting the Brits' capability to fight. Given more time, they feel they can get the occupiers out.

The rulers have not just India to worry about but the other colonies and the world wars. So there will be an opportunity to strike when the Empire weakens or becomes preoccupied with other things. Besides, there are many good and decent Britons who support the cause of independence – they can help spread the message among their citizens.

After you finish interviewing one such impressive strategic-thinking action-oriented proactive revolutionary, in walks a middle-aged, rather skinny man. He wears glasses and a loin-cloth, nothing else. Your first impressions: no physical presence, no gravitas.

"I'm Mohandas," he says by way of introduction.

You offer him a seat and get straight to the point, "Mohandas, how do you plan to fight the powerful Empire and get us independence?"

Mohandas says, "Through non-violence. I will appeal to the British sense of justice, decency, and fair-play."

Non-violence? Decency? Fair play? Doesn't he know we're talking about a fight for independence from a superpower?

"Mohandas, if the British had any decency, they would've left a long time back," you respond.

"Well, no one has actually asked them nicely to leave," Mohandas states.

"And you think if you ask nicely, they'll go?"

"It will take time, but they'll go in the end."

"You aren't even one of India's many kings, Mohandas. And these are powerful kings the British can squash without a thought. I don't think you quite appreciate just how powerful our rulers are. Why should they listen to you?"

"Because I'll reason with them peacefully."

"Ummm ... and how do you plan to inspire the masses with this novel idea of asking our rulers nicely to leave?"

"I won't inspire them. I will just do what I think is right. They can follow me if they wish."

By now you're thinking the man is insane. He has no idea what he's up against. Besides, he doesn't know what being a leader is. He's not at all proactive. How on earth can you just say, "I'll do what I think is right. If the rest want to follow me, fine"?

But you want to humor the man, so you ask, "And how do you plan to get the British out of here, besides asking nicely?"

"Through non-cooperation. I will disobey any laws that I think are unjust. But I will not raise a finger against them. I'll spend time in jail if that's what it takes."

"If you're in jail, how are you going to fight?" you ask, amazed.

"My fight is the fight of morality."

"Rightness over wrongness is your main weapon against an enemy which views our fight for independence as an insurgency?"

"Yes."

"Do you have any other weapons in mind, Mohandas?"

"Yes, *Satyagraha*: the force of truth, love, and non-violence. Also, I'll often starve myself by going on hunger strikes."

This man is off the scale. It would be amusing if the issue wasn't so serious.

"Get real!" you tell him. "And don't quit your day job."

You call security and tell the man, "Please make sure this Mohandas chap gets home safely. He needs help."

Mohandas Gandhi wasn't an elected leader. He could hardly be since the British ruled the country. But he had the backing of the vast majority of his people. People who took blows to their bodies and didn't retaliate, all because he said so. The rest is history.

The point is that Gandhi wouldn't have been Gandhi if he had been thrust upon India's people. What made him so powerful was the fact that Indians voluntarily accepted him as their leader. His leadership took two to tango – himself and the people of India. When it takes two to tango, you have a system.

Let's now take a look at the actions of a contemporary leader, a giant of our times called Nelson Mandela. It's always astounding to see how he emerged from a long spell of imprisonment with no sense of vengefulness against the White South African regime that jailed him or White South Africans themselves. How could he possibly be like this?

You will better understand his leadership when you learn about an African word, *Ubuntu*. While there's no direct translation of the word in the English language, one definition is that "a person is a person through other persons." This encompasses several meanings including compassion, openness, caring, trust, unselfishness, a spirit of generosity, a bond that is shared by all humanity, wholeness, and so on. The fundamental precept of *Ubuntu* is this: people are interconnected and interdependent. If you demean someone, you demean yourself. So your highest purpose should be to serve others, and in doing so, you serve yourself.

*Ubuntu* is also a great way of describing leadership as a system because if people are interconnected, you cannot talk about a leader in isolation. When you talk about a leader, you automatically bring other people into the equation. Mandela's efforts at reconciliation make a lot more sense once you look at his actions through the lens of *Ubuntu*. Mandela could hardly call himself a leader if he demeaned or took revenge against a section of his own people. As Archbishop Desmond Tutu said:

> If his people are going to be prosperous, he's got to be a good chief, and a chief is a chief through the people. ... It is a deep compassion which includes, as we have seen, those who have roughed him up. This "ubuntu" approach that ... ultimately if your humanity, if your personhood is enhanced, mine – ipso facto – is going to be enhanced as well."[23]

Only the greatest of leaders truly understand this. Consider what Mahatma Gandhi said: "It has always been a mystery to me how men can feel themselves honoured by the humiliation of their fellow beings." And Abraham Lincoln: "No man is good enough to govern another man without that other's consent." All the complex theories on what makes a great leader fall apart before Lincoln's crystal-clear understanding of leadership.

So if you want to be a real leader, you need to understand that leadership is a system. But it's not only leadership that's a system. Our organizations are systems too, because the organization's existence arises from the interactions between the people who work there. If the people worked alone and didn't interact, the organization would fall apart. So let's apply systems thinking to our offices, to find out what kind of systems we have at the place we spend most of our daylight – and often night-time – hours.

# 7

# SYSTEMS
# THINKING
# AT WORK

What do we do when there's a problem in our organizations? We try to pinpoint the source of the problem and repair it. In trying to pinpoint the problem, what are we doing? We're analyzing. We keep going through deeper and deeper levels of analysis.

In our frenzied analytical fervor to find fault, what do we find? We find an animal that appears over and over again: the scapegoat. This is natural because the smallest thing than can be analyzed in an organization is the individual. Although people often recognize that the "organizational culture" is defective, there's always an underlying subtext. That somehow, through some superhuman strength, the individual is supposed to over-come the organizational flaws. If individuals can't do this, or far worse, they have the audacity to talk about the flaws, they are unceremoniously thrown out.

Does dismissing an individual make any difference? Mostly, the answer is no. This is because the fault lies in our mindset: we look at the organization as a mechanical thing that can be taken apart and analyzed. We can do an excellent job of analysis, but analysis is the wrong tool for the job. Since it's the wrong tool for the job, we end up getting the wrong answers. And some unfortunate soul takes a hit.

What's the right tool, then? Since the workplace is a system, we need to examine it through the method appropriate for systems: systems thinking.

Actually, this is not as novel as it sounds. Many people have already recognized that organizations are entities in themselves and can have flaws in the way they function. Consultants have created a whole bouquet of buzzwords that they offer to company bosses by way of solving problems: organization restructuring, matrix management, business process reengineering, management by objectives (MBO), inverted pyramid, and so on.

One day, your CEO's pet consultant advises her, "To become more efficient and profitable, you need to restructure your organization, reduce headcount through downsizing, attrition or natural wastage, focus on your core-competences, outsource your non-core activities, matrix manage the change-management process, manage by objectives, and voila, you're home!"

But there's a tiny problem with that jargon-loaded solution: it doesn't mention real people. Where does that leave you? Or have they forgotten that George and Midori, and Rahul and Nasser, and Mary and Pierre, not robots, work at your company?

Much as you won't believe it, the consultants, your CEO and your top managers haven't forgotten you. They haven't forgotten that you're a human being. They haven't forgotten your boss is a human being. But as I've often mentioned, like us, they've been conditioned not to talk about it. Who would want to talk about the messy, complicated relationships involving bosses and subordinates? These relationships form the absolute core of any organization and are the wickedest problem of all. The boss–subordinate interaction not only defines the nature of the relationship between those two individuals, it also defines the nature of all relationships in an organization. How can all relationships be affected? All relationships are affected because the workplace is a system.

Why then, do experts and top managers not talk of fixing that core relationship – between a boss and a subordinate? Why do they always sidestep the issue that's fundamental to the way an organization works?

There are two main reasons. First, if it ain't broke, don't fix it. The boss–subordinate relationship isn't considered broken at all. Although you may beg to differ, it's considered normal because the phenomenon is so widespread. Moreover, we've gotten so accustomed to bad boss behavior that we've come to accept very low standards. Sociologist Diane Vaughan labels this acceptance of things that aren't supposed to happen as the "normalization of deviance."[24] In some ways this is a variation of the saying, "One fatal accident is a tragedy; a million, a statistic."

Second, it's just not appealing enough. Boss–subordinate problems are as old as the hills. That's how it's always been and that's how it will always be. Anyway, it just doesn't sound impressive enough to say, "We'll solve your boss troubles." Far grander to state, "We're organization transition consultants." It's sad, but the vast majority of these hard-working and well-meaning people are blinded by their own words. So they go around looking around for solutions in the wrong places.

These misguided approaches do not attack the basic attribute of a system: people and the interactions between them. People and their interactions are wicked problems because you can't just fix individuals' behaviors without reference to the system in which they work. So you can't apply a tame solution to a wicked problem. Nonetheless, we treat people as tame problems all the time and send them off on "leadership" or "teamwork" training courses to "fix" them. No wonder people are frustrated and unhappy. No wonder most of these efforts are doomed to fail.

So to figure out why bosses behave the way they do, and why you behave the way you do with your boss, we need to look at what kind of system we have at the workplace. Once we figure out what kind of system it is, we can then look at how this system impacts your boss's behavior and your behavior.

## What kind of system do we have at work?

To understand this, we need to return to our definition of leader:

*Leader:* A person who is elected by the people he or she is leading. *Corollary:* A person who leads without being elected is a dictator.

As we know, people make judgments all the time about someone's leadership ability without checking with the people he or she is going to lead. And those judgments are usually on the basis of that person's skills or personality. We say things like "He's got a commanding presence," "She's a real go-getter," "He's a great communicator," "She leads from the front," and so on. But these do not define leadership at all. They just define the individual's skills in certain areas. But on the basis of these skills, people are deemed to be leaders and promoted all the time.

Are these people really leaders? You now know they're not because they haven't been elected. By definition, they're dictators. Since the dictators and their subordinates interact, we have a system. What kind of system is this? A dictatorship system. Just as leadership is a system, dictatorship is a system too. But how does your boss become a dictator?

## How your boss becomes a dictator

How are bosses made? Usually, it goes something like this: someone is great at sales, so they promote him to being the leader of the sales team. Someone is terrific at designing, so she's promoted to becoming the head of a bunch of designers. Someone is wonderful at software development, so they make him the manager of several programmers.

Thus promotion to people management is actually this: a reward that puts someone in charge of people, for good work in an area unrelated to the leadership of people.

And when you get a new boss, how does that happen? You're simply told, "Scott will be your manager. You will report to Scott." Scott now has power over you. It's very innocuous and subtle, and there's no big drama.

But what has really happened? *Scott is now automatically a dictator because you don't have voting rights over him.* By definition, Scott is not a leader but a dictator.

No one suspects it, but the absence of voting rights results in a dictatorship system springing into existence. In other words, *inaction – not voting for your leader – results in a dictatorship system.* Because it's so easy to overlook, I call it a *stealth dictatorship system.* Anyone who has authority over you, without your having a say, is a *stealth dictator.* What does that make you? A *stealth subject.* This holds true for any situation – whether it's a full-time job, a temporary assignment, an hour-long meeting, or a one-minute conversation.

You probably think that labeling all bosses as dictators is grossly overstating the case, an exercise in witch-hunting or at best, a little too harsh. Not all bosses behave terribly, not all bosses are malevolent, not all bosses are ogres. In fact, many bosses are nice, friendly, and genuinely good people. How can we possibly call these decent people dictators? Hold on a bit, and let's examine something called "state of being."

## The boss's "state of being"

On the face of it, we cannot and should not label nice bosses as dictators. "Dictator" is a very harsh word, conjuring up images that aren't suitable for family viewing or language that's not meant for family listening. But dig a little deeper and you'll see this holds true only if we use the wrong measuring standard. While niceness or multiple abilities may sound like the right standard, it's actually the wrong one.

Before measuring your boss by her actions, you've got to measure her by her state of being. What's that supposed to mean? A state of being is not a feeling. It's not "I'm feeling angry" or "I'm feeling happy." Nor is it a character trait: "He's nice" or "He's compassionate." It's more like "I'm a husband," or "I'm a teacher," or "I'm a lawyer," or "I'm a mother." It's virtually your identity in a given context.

What's your boss's state of being relative to you? That of being a person with power over you, the state of being of a dictator. All boss behavior arises from that state of being. As long as that state of being is present, the rest becomes mere detail.

You may argue that it makes sense for the dictator state of being to be present. After all, since the boss and the subordinate are both conscious of the power equation, they watch their behaviors. The boss doesn't become too familiar and the subordinates don't take liberties. If you're a boss, you're always aware of the constant tug-of-war between trying to be friendly, but not too friendly. Subordinates feel the same tug-of-war and always try to ensure they don't overstep the mark.

The tug-of-war seems an indicator of healthy tension. But it's not that simple. The biggest problem with the presence of the boss state of being – however nice the boss – is this: It's a dormant volcano. Unlike an active volcano for which precautionary measures can be taken, a dormant volcano one just lays there, lurking. Then, when conditions are just right – and I'll talk about these conditions later – the volcano erupts. No one, including the boss, may be prepared for it. This "boss eruption" doesn't necessarily mean an explosion of anger or fury. It's an explosion of boss behavior in any of its forms. The consequences can be devastating – not just for the people involved, but for the organization as well.

Here's what I mean. Take two people, Jerry and Sara, who've known each other for years. Jerry is very mild by nature and wouldn't hurt a fly. In all the time that Sara has known him, he's never yelled or screamed at her. Jerry isn't secretly in love with Sara and neither is she secretly in love with him. One day, Sara tells Jerry that she's having a relationship with another man. Jerry explodes. He's not angry about the person she's having a relationship with, he's furious simply because she's having a relationship with someone else.

Jerry's behavior is obviously "bad." Jerry may have his opinions, but it's not his place to tell Sara how to run her life. Despite all this, she doesn't seem surprised by Jerry's behavior. In fact, she is quite prepared for it. What's going on?

I now tell you that Jerry is Sara's husband. Jerry loves his wife dearly, and she's often told him she loves him dearly too. They've been happily married for several years and Jerry is quietly proud of the fact that his marriage is held up as an example to all. Then Sara drops the bombshell that she's having an affair.

In the light of this new information, does Jerry's "out of character" behavior surprise you? No. Is Sara surprised? No. You're not surprised because you know that Jerry's state of being in relation to Sara is "husband." They live in a "system" called marriage. Under normal circumstances, Jerry is a loving husband. But in a certain situation – he finds out his wife is having an affair – another aspect of "husbandhood" erupts.

In contrast, if we answered, "Who is a husband?" with traits such as "emotionally equable" or "protective," we wouldn't understand Jerry's behavior. But with the definition of a husband as "a married man," his behavior instantly falls into place.

It's not just bosses who can have eruptions. Your state of being in relation to your boss is as a subject. Every time you keep quiet when you know you should be speaking up is an example of subject behavior. Your subject state of being is another dormant volcano. It can erupt at any time. And that's dangerous too, as we'll see later.

So we need to understand that it doesn't take awful behavior by a boss to qualify him or her as dictator. It only takes a state of being.

Now that we know that all bosses are dictators, let's look at how they behave. Well, we already know how they behave. But do they just exhibit their individual traits, or does something else cause their dictatorial behavior?

# 8

# HOW DOES
# DICTATORIAL
# BEHAVIOR ARISE?

As we've seen earlier, the strange thing about bosses is that apparently normal, nice, and decent people suddenly turn into proper bosses. In the face of these bosses, normally assertive and confident individuals turn into frightened and compliant sheep. How does this happen? To find out, let's get deeper into systems thinking, starting with something called "emergent properties". (Please don't doze off the moment you see staid terms like "systems thinking" or "emergent properties" – boring though these words sound, they're going to show us what really goes on at our offices.)

## Emergent properties

There's a concept in systems thinking called emergent properties. What this means is that when individual parts of a system interact, they produce characteristics that are different from the characteristics of the individual parts.

Generally, you can't predict the emergent properties from knowing the characteristics of the individual components. For example, hydrogen and oxygen are gases in their natural state. When the gases interact they produce water, with "wetness" being an emergent property. In trying to predict wetness, you could analyze hydrogen or oxygen as much as you wanted, but you would never find wetness in either of them. These gases are programmed to produce wetness only when they interact.

Similarly, the emergent property of an aircraft is flight. When you're on a plane that's taking off, it may seem that the engines are groaning under the strain of getting such a heavy object off the ground. However, the reality is that beyond a certain speed, the plane has no choice but to take off. It can't do anything but fly.

Flight is an outcome of the aircraft parts interacting with each other and the atmospheric air. But on their own, the individual parts cannot fly. And just by knowing the properties of the individual parts, you cannot predict that the aircraft will fly. You can analyze the plane – the wings, the tail, or the engines – as much as you want, but you will not be able to find the property of flight in any of them.

Marriage is also a system that has its own emergent properties. When two people are courting – a kind of interaction, you have a "courtship" system with "lover boy" and "lover girl." This system produces one kind of behavior. Then lover boy and lover girl get married. The new system is called marriage, and the couple are now husband and wife. The system of marriage produces different behaviors from the courtship system. Before marriage, lover boy and lover girl could be completely non-confrontational people with mild or non-existent tempers. They get married and the arguments start. They wonder what's going on because they don't recognize themselves any more. That's what systems do to you – they bring out behaviors that may not have existed before the interaction.

Unfortunately, people often expect courtship system behaviors to continue in a marriage system. It doesn't work that way because courtship and marriage are two different systems that produce two different behaviors. The inevitable result of expecting one system's behavior in another system? Frustration, disappointment, or divorce. So we've got it all wrong: marriage may be an institution, but it's really a system.

What does this have to do with bosses? Remember that leadership is a system in which two components interact – the leader and the individual being led. By definition, your boss is a dictator and you are a subject. The system is that of a dictatorship. So let's look for the emergent properties in a dictatorship system. Where do we find such systems so that we can go and take a look?

Actually, it's not hard. These systems go by names you're already familiar with: names such as Libya, Iran, Russia, Sudan, Syria, Algeria, North Korea, Zimbabwe, Pakistan, China, Saudi Arabia, and many others that you know of.

What's the predominant emergent property in dictatorship systems? It's that dreaded four-letter word: *fear*. Other emergent properties in dictatorship systems include:

- lack of freedom
- poverty
- lack of competitive advantage
- exodus of talented people (who leave if they can)
- media censorship
- little or no innovation
- a culture of secrecy and a lack of trust
- rigid hierarchy.

It's often said about war that "Truth is the first casualty." The same is true of dictatorships. No one wants to tell the truth because to survive, everyone needs to live in the dictator's deluded world. Even if that means people lying to themselves.

In a dictatorship, the people are not citizens but subjects literally. Their very existence is subject to the ruler's whims and fancies. There is a clearly defined hierarchy with those close to the dictator sitting luxuriously on the high rungs, and the commoners struggling to survive on the bottom rungs. Status on the power ladder is everything.

How do people in dictatorships know they should be scared? No one tells them that because they don't have the right to vote, they should behave fearfully. Yet, they do. What this reveals is that fearful behavior is an emergent property – an automatic result of the system the subjects live in. You may as well have programmed the subjects to behave fearfully.

For dictators, the emergent property is absolute power. No one needs to tell a dictator that because his subjects can't vote, he can behave dictatorially. He just does. He tortures, oppresses, humiliates, or kills. The ruler considers himself literally and viscerally superior to everyone else. This behavior is automatic; it may as well have been programmed.

These emergent properties show up regardless of apparent differences. Systems such as Algeria, Myanmar (Burma), North Korea, Zimbabwe, and Libya have peoples with vastly differing traditions, languages, and ethnicities. Despite these differences, they are all very much alike – they are closed and fearful societies. They're also poor and uncompetitive. To be blunt, these systems are losers.

Let's look at the opposite scenario now: leadership systems, and the emergent properties for those systems. Again, you're already familiar with many leadership systems – they go by names such as the United States, Britain, France, Canada, Australia, France, Holland, Italy, Germany, Japan, and so on.

What's the predominant emergent property in these systems? The answer is a singularly profound word: *freedom.*

You could argue that we have the right to vote only because we're free. To prevent a chicken and egg situation here, let me ask the opposite question: if we did not have the right to vote, would we continue to be free? The answer is no.

How do people with voting rights know they can behave freely? Who tells them? No one. They just behave freely, within the boundaries they set for themselves. They criticize their leaders, ridicule them, change them, praise them, or whatever. Citizens take initiatives and act without having to get permission from their leader for every little thing. There is a culture of dynamism and openness.

In turn, the rulers, though vested with power, behave as leaders. The citizens and the leaders behave in ways that are products of the system. These behaviors are so automatic, they may as well be programmed.

Further, where there's freedom, leadership is considered a job just like any other job. Unlike monarchs or dictators who consider themselves inherently superior to commoners, leaders are not considered superior to citizens. Yes, leadership is a very highly regarded job, but it's still a job. If a leader isn't performing to our expectations, we can throw him or her out.

Many other things emerge when people have the right to vote:

- innovation
- wealth
- power
- competitive advantage
- free media
- attraction of talent (via immigration)
- culture of openness.

The richest and most powerful systems on the planet are those in which people vote for their leaders – the United States being a prime example. You could argue that communist China is becoming powerful too – the answer is yes of course, but its ascent began only after it gave its citizens more economic freedom. In any case, a better question to ask is: how much more rich and powerful would China be, if its citizens had the right to vote?

Or you could argue that systems such as Saudi Arabia are wealthy. But we know that Saudi's wealth comes not from its people but its oil. Besides, the country lives only at the mercy of a far more powerful free system, the United States.

You could also debate that in a system like India, where people do have voting rights, poverty is widespread. But there's a historical reason for this – because of rapacious British colonialism (dictatorial control over India), the country associated capitalism with subjugation. India thus strangled the economic freedom of its own people for decades. Once the economic handcuffs came off in the early 1990s, it began to get competitive and wealthy, a journey that still continues.

The important point here is that real freedom brings real success. Shared systems matter more than shared national cultures. For example, Japan, Germany, Italy, France, Britain, and the United States are all very different from one another. Their peoples have different histories, traditions, languages, and even ethnicities. Yet, despite these huge differences, they are amazingly similar – they are free, wealthy, innovative and powerful. Winning is an emergent property. These systems are winners.

So the moral of the story is this: freedom works, fear doesn't.

Having looked at emergent properties in country systems, let's now look at emergent properties at the workplace. You may say there's a big difference between a country and an organization or company. But remember that fundamentally, leadership is simply the interaction between the leader and the led. The interaction is the main thing. So let's examine the emergent properties in our offices – in which people don't have the right to vote for their bosses.

(For the rest of this book, I'll be using the terms leadership systems and free systems interchangeably; the same goes for dictatorship systems and fear systems.)

# 9

# EMERGENT PROPERTIES AT THE OFFICE

How do people behave at work? Subordinates are afraid to criticize their bosses, even in private, similar to dictatorships where people are scared to criticize their rulers. Just like courtiers or sycophants in monarchies or dictatorships, subordinates continually strive to be in the good books of their superiors.

There's often a culture of secrecy. In stark similarity with dictatorships, there's censorship – you don't see cartoons or articles by subordinates criticizing their bosses splashed routinely in the in-house magazine or the company intranet. You had better stick to the party line or you're asking for trouble.

So what's the predominant emergent property for subordinates? Fear. This could range from feeling occasionally anxious to being continually apprehensive to living in complete and abject terror.

As we've seen earlier, when oxygen and hydrogen interact, the product is water, with wetness being a "natural" emergent property. In contrast, much-heavier-than-air planes are consciously engineered to produce the emergent property called flight. And in contrast to consciously engineered airplanes, we've unconsciously engineered the workplace system such that when a boss and subordinate interact, fear is an emergent property. In effect, subordinates are programmed to behave fearfully.

Haven't you ever felt fearful – or even mildly anxious at times – in relation to your boss? You may think fear is too strong a word. But as always, a couple of inquisitive professors have done some research into this phenomenon. The professors, Amy Edmondson of Harvard Business School and James Detert of Penn State, researched how people in large corporations behave when dealing with those in positions of power.

In particular, they examined a phenomenon they call "latent voice episodes."[25] These are instances when people have something to say, but don't. These episodes are "latent" because they are potential communication – communication that may or may not happen. They wrote about this in a paper called "Latent voice episodes: the situation-specific nature of speaking up at work."

In plain language, the professors researched why people don't speak up to their bosses. "Up" is the operative word here, because the professors talk about something called "upward voice." This "voice" is communication that's directed to someone higher up the hierarchy – someone with more power than the speaker.

Why don't people speak up? The professors say it's because of fear: "Perhaps most surprising to us has been the degree to which fear appears to be a feature of modern work life."

In our apparently flat and supposedly free workplace, why are people so fearful? The professors explain:

> Turning to the modern economy, most of us depend on hierarchical organisations and their agents (i.e., bosses) to meet many of our basic needs for economic support and human relationships. Thus, fear of offending those above us is both natural and widespread.

By the way, the word "bosses" in brackets is not something I've put in. It's a part of their quote.

Plainly put, we're scared because we need the money and we need the people. No wonder we keep our mouths shut. It's important to note the professors talk about the "modern" economy. What's the big deal about the word "modern"? Because we're modern economies, we're not supposed to be scared of "speaking up" to our bosses. What does modernity imply? More than anything else, modernity implies freedom. No society is considered modern if it's not free.

So we have a paradox – we have people in modern, free countries afraid to speak up to their bosses. Why? It's because the workplace is not modern. It's primitive. As you leave the street and enter your office, you cross the threshold that marks the boundary between freedom and fear. Your state of being changes from that of a free citizen to a fearful subject.

What else does this fear result in? Subordinates do what people in fear systems do. They behave passively and don't take the initiative. The professors state, "Employees aren't failing to provide ideas or input because they've 'checked out' and just don't care, but because of fear."

Why do subordinates often end up doing only what their boss tells them to do, and not provide ideas or input? Why do team members just sit there and wait for orders? Evidently, they must be either morons or slackers.

But strangely, these very same people can transform into completely different people the minute they step out of the office. They turn into dynamic individuals, enjoying hobbies or community activities. They take initiatives, plan strategies and do all the things they aren't doing at the office. What's going on?

While they're free outside the office, the workplace system has actually taught them to become helpless inside the office. There's a theory called "learned helplessness" developed by psychologist Martin Seligman.[26] According to this theory, people become apathetic or submissive when they're put in situations in which they experience pain, harm, and captivity, and there's no possibility of escape. So they feel powerless and don't try to break out or improve the situation even if an opportunity presents itself.

Essentially, "learned helplessness" is about individuals' inability to control their environment. When individuals feel they have no control, they stop trying even in the face of continued pain. Instead of a "can do" attitude, they develop a "can't do" attitude.

Symptoms of learned helplessness include fatigue, fearfulness, anxiety, loss of appetite, a lack of confidence, and impaired ability to think clearly and solve problems. In fact, learned helplessness can be a cause for depression.

People in dictatorships suffer from learned helplessness. They passively accept their fate because they've seen the pain associated with taking action – purges in which millions are killed, tortured, kidnapped, and so on. Unsurprisingly, people stop trying to do anything.

Of course, we don't suffer as harshly at the office. Having said that, many people feel trapped under a bad boss – they feel they can't quit for financial or other reasons, and neither can they fight back. They've seen colleagues humiliated or abused by the boss and perhaps they've been targets themselves. These are traumatic events, which no one wants to experience. Hence it's not surprising that subordinates do the bare minimum to ensure survival, with behaviors that closely resemble those of subjects in dictatorships. The inevitable result is that subordinates suffer from anxiety, fatigue and other symptoms of learned helplessness that we lump together under that all-conquering label, stress.

There's something else that can cause a lot of stress: change. If people want to confront their boss, they are effectively trying to change the status quo. They are going to go through a lot of stress. They are taking on the massive task of fighting the existing rulers and power structure. Worse, they are going to have to take responsibility for their actions. This is not at all easy. Hence, as Sally Bibb says in *The Stone Age Company*:

> It is not just the people at the top of the tree, those with power, who don't want to change. Despite the fact that many people complain about and laugh at their bosses, many of them don't want things to change either. There is a certain comfort in the system of hierarchy. We can blame those at the top, as well as handing over all responsibility to them when things go wrong.[27]

If the main emergent property for subordinates is fear in any of its forms, what is it for bosses? You guessed it: absolute power. The result? Bosses behave like dictators. They behave like dictators because they are dictators. It's an automatic result of the system the bosses are in. In effect, your boss is programmed to be a dictator.

Like dictators who torture and bully people just for the fun of it, so do bosses. An article in the *New York Times* cites a study by Dr Harvey A. Hornstein, a retired professor at Columbia University and the author of the book *Brutal Bosses and their Prey*.[28] Dr Hornstein found that while bosses used power in expected ways like putting down threatening subordinates or making them scapegoats, their main reason for abusing power was far more monstrous. Managers abused their subordinates for the fun of it, for the sheer pleasure of exercising power. Dr. Hornstein was quoted, "It was a kind of low-grade sadism, that was the most common reason. They'd start on one person and then move onto someone else." Dr Gary Namie, director of an institute called the Workplace Bullying and Trauma Institute, was quoted as saying that women are at least as likely as men to be the aggressors, and they are more likely to be targets.

It's not just that bosses are dictators. The whole workplace system is that of a dictatorship; relationships between subordinates suffer too. As in dictatorships, subordinates who witness a colleague being humiliated are relieved that they aren't the target, and feel happy that they look good in comparison. The *NYT* article also mentions a survey by Dr Michelle Duffy, a psychologist at the University of Kentucky Business School. The survey found that although workers were happy when praised by their boss, they were happier when the praise was accompanied by news that a colleague was struggling. So much for teamwork.

Dr Duffy also noted that co-workers watch silently when a colleague is being humiliated. The person at the receiving end feels isolated, while those who idly witness the humiliation ease their guilt by making up reasons for the colleague's shaming – perhaps he was lazy or did something to deserve it. And like all small-time dictators, bosses who enjoy abusing power offer reverence to those with even more power – their own superiors.

There are other knock-on effects too. Dr Leigh Thompson, an organizational psychologist at Kellogg Business School, and Cameron Anderson of the New York University Business School, studied the effects of management styles on small groups. In a simulation, they found that a bullying, "alpha dog" boss transformed the behavior of the number two managers, who themselves became copies of their bullying boss.

The startling thing was that as in the Stanford Prison Experiment, this behavior happened even if the number 2 managers were rated as compassionate on personality tests outside the experiment. Because they wanted to please their bosses, the number 2 managers temporarily turned into copies of their bosses. This phenomenon also worked the other way: if the boss was compassionate, the number 2 managers became compassionate too. But in both cases, the people at level 3 were completely subject to what was going on at levels 1 and 2.

Levels reflect a strict hierarchy, which is a defining characteristic of dictatorships and monarchies. People know their place and are expected to behave accordingly. A hierarchy is also the defining characteristic of a contemporary organization chart. This top-down thinking is revealed in the words we use: "superior" for our bosses, and "subordinates" for those below us.

Say a spaceship lands in your backyard. In true movie style, a ladder emerges and an alien steps out. You're a brave person, so you walk towards the alien. The alien then says to you, "Take me to your superior."

Superior? Why are you surprised? You're surprised because the alien seems to want to meet your boss. You were expecting "Take me to your leader," weren't you? If the alien thinks your leader is your superior, it's got another thing coming. You'd give the alien a big lecture on why the leader of your country is most definitely not your superior. But at the office, that's another story altogether.

The words "superior" and "subordinate" indicate your status as a human being itself, not just your expertise. Moreover, your position is graded, say on an ascending scale of 1–12. The person at grade 11 is higher ranked than the person at grade 7. What's the objective of this grading? To put you in your place.

The world's most powerful man is far above your station. But you are not frightened of openly calling the US President an idiot. Why then are you afraid of openly calling your boss an idiot? You're scared because the moment you enter your workplace, you leave a free system and enter a dictatorship system. Since you "know your place," you behave with your boss and those who are higher up, as a person of lower status behaves with a superior – submissively and with a measure of anxiety. Obviously, we often do this in extremely sophisticated ways.

If we draw a table placing the emergent properties of a dictatorship system, a workplace system, and a leadership system side by side, the similarities and differences become clear.

| Emergent properties | | |
|---|---|---|
| **Dictatorship system** | **Workplace system** | **Free system** |
| For subjects, fear is the prevalent emotion | For subordinates, fear/anxiety is the prevalent emotion | Citizens are fearless |
| Dictators have absolute power | Bosses wield a tremendous amount of power over subordinates | Leaders do not have absolute power; they are subject to various controls |
| Criticism of leaders forbidden in public or private. Consequences of criticism can be harsh: execution | Criticism of boss not explicitly forbidden, but since the consequences can be harsh (being fired), subordinates don't criticize their bosses openly | Leaders are routinely criticized, openly and in public |
| No free press/media. Strict censorship enforced by administration, self-censorship by subjects | No free in-house press/media. No one even dreams of writing critical articles of their bosses for the in-house magazine | Media/press is completely free |
| The dictator can choose the degree to which he or she empowers subjects: freedom is not institutionalized | Bosses can choose the degree to which they empower subordinates: freedom is not institutionalized. | The system empowers citizens: freedom is institutionalized |

| Emergent properties (continued) | | |
|---|---|---|
| **Dictatorship system** | **Workplace system** | **Free system** |
| Dissent is not tolerated | Dissent tolerated to the extent the boss wants to tolerate it. When subordinates doubt whether or not the boss will tolerate dissent, they will not do it | Dissent is built into the system by the mechanism of having an opposition |
| Leaders behave as tyrants. They can, and do, abuse their subjects | Bosses can behave arbitrarily – they can, and do abuse their subordinates – either emotionally, or in extreme cases, physically | Leaders, though vested with power, treat citizens with respect. |
| Subjects try to keep themselves in their dictator's good books | Subordinates try to keep themselves in their boss's good books | Leaders try to keep themselves in their citizens' good books |
| Subjects suffer from learned helplessness | Subordinates suffer from learned helpless – don't take as much initiative as they perhaps can | Citizens are perpetually taking initiatives |
| Culture of secrecy: subjects aren't always told what's going on | Culture of secrecy: employees aren't always told what's going on | Freedom of information is a right of citizens |

| Emergent properties (continued) | | |
|---|---|---|
| **Dictatorship system** | **Workplace system** | **Free system** |
| No recourse to justice: the dictator is the law | No recourse to justice: the boss is the law. | Leader can be voted out or impeached |
| Dictator decides whether or not you qualify as a "good" subject. If he or she decides that you aren't, you can be executed. Your fate, however "good" you are, is in the dictator's hands | Boss evaluates you via your annual appraisal, and decides if you are a "good" employee. If he or she decides that you aren't, you can be fired. Your fate is in the boss's hands | Your leader's fate is in the citizens' hands |

The fundamental point is that in a dictatorship system, power is the ultimate status symbol. You show off your status by showing off your power. And subordinates show respect to that power by bowing down to you, metaphorically if not literally. Even in Western cultures.

# 10

# POWER:
# THE ULTIMATE
# STATUS SYMBOL

There's a myth that subordinates in Western cultures are less status driven, that they're less deferential to bosses than their Eastern counterparts. While Westerners are perhaps less deferential to authority figures outside the office, inside the office they're no different from Easterners. This deferential behavior is masked by the apparently "flat" social interactions in which the boss is called by first name rather than "sir" or "ma'am," there's no obvious bowing, and subordinates don't stand when the boss enters. But just below the surface of this superficially "equal" behavior lurks a strong undercurrent of submissiveness.

While Westerners are relatively irreverent to authority outside the office, how can they be deferential to bosses inside the office? The answer lies in the individualistic model of leadership. Individualism is very highly prized in Western, particularly US, societies. The leader is positioned as a supremely independent and confident person, in the manner of a rugged gunslinger brought into a Wild West town to sort out its problems.

Hence, the Western model of leadership pays homage to the leader as someone who proactively takes charge and is a real action-hero go-getter. A leader is most definitely not someone who approaches his or her would-be team and politely asks first, "May I have your permission to lead you?" Take-charge behavior this is not.

Given the need to visibly stamp his authority, a gunslinger is unlikely to tolerate dissent or challenges to his position. Western bosses have exactly this attitude, which, although similar to the attitude of Eastern bosses, has a different origin. Eastern bosses expect to be obeyed by virtue of their position in the hierarchy. In contrast, Western bosses are conditioned to continually "prove" their leadership through a tough and imposing attitude. In both Eastern and Western cases, the result is the same: submissive subordinates.

If subordinates don't easily submit, they're slotted into the category called the "boss hater." Jack Welch, GE's ex-chief gunslinger, says in his book *Winning*, "Boss haters are a real breed. It doesn't make any difference who these people work for, they go into any authority relationship with barely repressed cynicism. ... Boss haters usually exude constant low-level negativity toward 'the system.'"[29]

We nod our heads in agreement. We know that boss haters exist, and it's a pain to be around them because they're always complaining. They have problems with authority and often mess up things for others.

But let's flip that boss-hater sentence around so that it now reads: "Freedom-lovers are a real breed. It doesn't make any difference which dictators these people work for, they usually go into any authority relationship with barely repressed cynicism. ... Freedom-lovers usually exude constant low-level negativity toward the 'system.'"

Not so easy now to go nodding your head with Mr Welch, is it?

Authority relationships are based on fear, not freedom. Boss haters have actually got it spot-on – they don't target individual bosses because they have somehow sensed the system is at fault.

Dissidents are always causing trouble for everyone's consciences because they're constantly looking for a better way. Colleagues know in their gut that the dissidents are right, but they don't want to jeopardize their positions by joining the fight. Better to tell these irritating folks to be quiet and sit down.

There's also an underlying assumption that boss-haters have a problem taking orders. But the issue is not about taking orders. The issue is *who* you take orders from. Is the person giving the orders a leader or a dictator?

It's not that all organizations are clueless. It's not that they aren't aware that hierarchical systems can do stupid things. Despite the lure of power, we also feel the need to hide it. So organizations use various tricks to reduce the effects of hierarchy – flattening organizations by reducing the number of layers between the top and bottom and so on.

One popular way of solving the problem is the job-title name game. I've talked about this before, but now that you're familiar with systems thinking, you'll be able to grasp even more firmly as to why changing labels doesn't really work.

## The job-title name-game

Many organizations feel the command-and-control mindset comes from the use of words such as "boss," "manager," "supervisor" or "superior." To get around this hierarchic mindset, organizations replace the old-style top-down words with new ones such as team leader or some version of "first among equals." Does this make any difference? As always, it's best to check what happens in real life.

Chances are that you have a team leader at work. You probably call your leader by her first name, say Susan. Just because you call her Susan, are you less aware that she's your boss? No way. You're always aware that she has power over you. And you behave accordingly.

Now let's say Susan decides she wants to sound far more important than just plain old "Susan." She's the boss of several people, after all. So she wants a more powerful title, one that will more accurately reflect her true glory. She decides to call herself "The Supreme Potentate of the Entire Universe." From now on, you will have to address her as "Your Most Esteemed Royal Highness." If you think that's crazy, Susan decides to do something crazier: she gives you the right to vote for her – so you can vote her out if you so wish.

Compare these two situations:

■ You get to call your boss by her first name but you don't get to vote for her.
■ You have to address your boss as "Your Most Esteemed Royal Highness." But you get the right to vote her out.

Which of the two situations would you prefer? In which of the two situations do you think you would have more freedom and less fear?

If you're still thinking, check out some real-life dictators who provide some excellent – and bizarre – examples of job-title mania. For instance, at one extreme, we have the late Idi Amin, former ruler of the African country Uganda. Amin made no bones about being an absolute despot and unashamedly called himself (see if you can read it out in a single breath):

> His Excellency President for Life, Field Marshal Al Hadji Doctor Idi Amin, VC, DSO, MC, Lord of All the Beasts of the Earth and Fishes of the Sea, and Conqueror of the British Empire in Africa in General and Uganda in Particular.[30]

At least Amin was honest and didn't try hiding behind user-friendly and freedom-implying labels such as president or prime minister. Like most dictators, Amin slaughtered hundreds of thousands of his fellow-countrymen. In the process, Uganda all but collapsed.

While Amin was one extreme, at the other extreme we have North Korea's dictator, Kim Jong Il, who calls himself quite pleasantly and succinctly, "Dear Leader."[31] Does "Dear Leader" behave any differently from Amin or other dictators? Hardly. Jong and his father "Great Leader" Kim Il Sung tortured and massacred thousands of their own citizens, and killed millions more by starving them. The result – a weak, impoverished country.

Though the job titles of Jong and Amin couldn't be more different, their behaviors couldn't be more similar. Between the two extremes in job-titling that Amin and Jong represent, we have some garden-variety dictators who give themselves a variety of designations. Depending on his mood, Pakistan's dictator calls himself president or chief executive. Cuba's dictator calls himself president. Saudi Arabia's dictator calls himself king. Other titles that have been used by dictators include chairman (China's "Chairman Mao") and general secretary (the ex-Soviet Union's dictators). The bottom line is that although the dictators' titles are varied, the results are the same: dictatorship systems and fear.

If job titles don't make any difference in fear systems, they don't make a difference in free systems either. For example, the US leader is called President, Germany's leader is called Chancellor and the UK's leader is called Prime Minister. You aren't supposed to address the US President as George, and neither can you address the UK Prime Minister as Tony. You call them "Mister President" and "Honorable Prime Minister." Does this make any difference as far as freedom is concerned? Not at all. People behave freely in all these countries.

The point is that just by changing job titles or using first names to gloss over the workplace fear system, the underlying reality doesn't change. It's still old wine in a new bottle. In fact, the situation is worse with "better" job titles or first names. This is because you look at the new titles and you naively expect new wine – freedom. So you behave freely and before you know it, the workplace system hits back at you. You're stunned, and you learn a harsh lesson: a boss by any other name behaves the same.

The Soviets went around calling everyone "comrade" in a bid to completely flatten the differences in status, just as some companies these days go around calling everyone "associate." Does that make any difference? No; the *Pygmalion* effect doesn't work because the system is far more powerful than the label.

As we've seen, emergent properties at the workplace resemble the emergent properties of a dictatorship. If you disagree, perhaps you're not even aware of what's going on. Still not convinced? Let's look for proof in the one place that knows exactly what goes on inside you: your body.

# 11

# THE MEDICAL
# EVIDENCE

Who's most at risk of getting heart disease, even taking into account lifestyle factors such as smoking, diet, exercise, and so on? We normally assume that it's the highly ambitious, highly driven, and apparently highly stressed out Type A personalities perched atop our organizational hierarchies.

But scientists have found the opposite. A couple of landmark studies, called the Whitehall studies,[32] dispelled the myth that "people in high status jobs have higher risks of heart disease." The Whitehall studies, named *Whitehall* and *Whitehall II*, examined the health of thousands of British civil servants over a period of decades.

The researchers said, "Conventional wisdom has it that a stressful job is one characterised by a high degree of responsibility and pressure. New research, to which *Whitehall II* has contributed, notably shows that that is incorrect."[33]

The studies found that rather than work pressure, it was a person's position in the organization hierarchy that was directly related to the risk of heart disease. The studies found that "[M]en in the lowest employment grades were much more likely to die prematurely than men in the highest grades. [T]he more senior you are in the employment hierarchy, the longer you might expect to live compared to people in lower employment grades."[34]

Note that, "This is particularly interesting when we reflect that the Civil Service excludes the richest and poorest members of society."[35] In other words, although those on the lower rungs are not dirt poor, they still die before their higher-ups.

According to the director of the *Whitehall II* study, Sir Michael Marmot:

> It was not the case that people in high stress jobs had a higher risk of heart attack, rather it went exactly the other way: people at the bottom of the hierarchy had a higher risk of heart attacks.[36]
>
> Secondly, it was a social gradient. The lower you were in the hierarchy, the higher the risk. So it wasn't top versus bottom, but it was graded. People who are in the middle range have more disease than people at the top. People in the lower part of the middle range have more disease than those who are in the upper part of the middle range, and people at the bottom have more disease than those in the middle range. And, thirdly, the social gradient applied to all the major causes of death.

The social gradient was observed for a range of illnesses: heart disease, some cancers, chronic lung disease, gastrointestinal disease, depression, suicide, back pain, and general feelings of being unwell.[37]

The study also found that within grades, there was hardly any difference between men and women.[38]

Why does position in the hierarchy matter so much? The issue the Whitehall researchers studied was job control. The higher you were on the hierarchy, the more control you had; the lower you were, the less control you had. The studies state that it's low control rather than a job's high demands that can make you seriously ill: "An analysis of British occupational mortality suggested that high demands were less important predictors of mortality than low control. In the *Whitehall II* study people in the high grades, who have lower coronary risk, have higher demands than the low grades."[39]

Two factors went into measuring job control: the degree of authority over decisions and the use of skills.[40] Fundamentally, the Whitehall Study shows that the more power you have over your destiny at work, the less likely you are to suffer from major diseases. What does having power over your own destiny mean? In a word, freedom.

We can draw a diagram to represent the Whitehall study, in terms of the corporate pyramid.

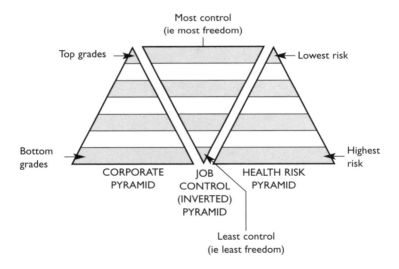

Let's look at this in the context of free and fear systems. If varying degrees of freedom at the office causes corresponding variations in the health of employees, it should follow that varying degrees of freedom among countries should cause corresponding variations in the health of their peoples.

It turns out that scientists have also studied this – they examined the effect of freedom (elected rulers, political rights, and civil liberties) on health. The study's sample represented 98 percent of the world's population in 170 countries. The study found: "The highest levels of health were in free countries followed by the partially free countries, and the worst levels of health were in countries that were not free."[41]

Thus, similar to the Whitehall findings, the effects of freedom are graded – your health varies according to the amount of freedom you have. If we juxtapose the Whitehall study and the freedom/health study, you'll see the similarities are striking:

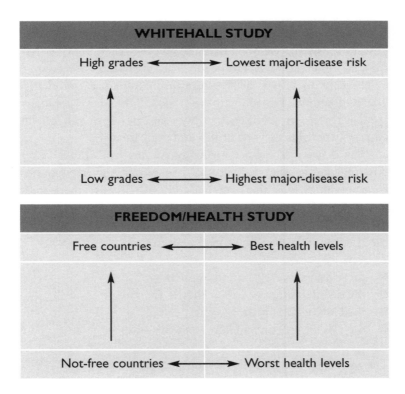

What does this show? That our bodies can tell the difference between living in freedom and living in fear. Using health as an indicator, we can infer that freedom varies according to grade or rank in the office hierarchy. Those in the lowest grades have less freedom than those in the highest grades. How different is this from a dictatorship where the dictator at the top of the hierarchy has the most freedom, and the people at the bottom have little or no freedom?

Nobody likes being powerless and if we are, it shows up in our bodies. Have you ever thought, "My blood pressure goes up whenever I see my boss"? You're not imagining things. A study showed that if a subordinate thought his or her boss was unfair, that subordinate's blood pressure went up every time the boss interacted with him or her.[42]

When does the issue of unfairness crop up? When someone has power over us and we don't have the power to fight back, we feel trapped. When do we feel trapped? When we have no freedom.

Perhaps in future, health insurance companies will charge you a premium according to your position on the company ladder. The lower you are, the more you pay – so you get hit twice where it hurts: your health and your finances.

But if insurers extract higher premiums from those lower down the ladder, they will also have to extract higher premiums from organizations that are hierarchical, because the consequences of hierarchy and dictatorship are disastrous not just for the body. They can be catastrophic for projects or organizations too. Let's look at four high-profile cases:

- the world's worst aviation accident
- the disintegration of Space Shuttle *Challenger*
- the *Columbia* Shuttle disaster
- the US-led war on Saddam Hussein's Iraq.

The events span a period of almost three decades, from 1977 to 2003. You'll see that despite all the talk of organizational re-engineering and what have you, organizations haven't fundamentally changed in all that time. And tragically, the results have stayed the same too.

# Section

## III

### The Consequences
### of Dictatorship

# 12

# ONE JUMBO JET SMASHES INTO ANOTHER

On a foggy Sunday afternoon in March 1977, a Boeing 747 jumbo jet belonging to the Dutch airline KLM began its take-off run. Because of dense fog and low-lying clouds, the pilots couldn't see too far ahead. As his plane gathered speed, the captain suddenly noticed a jumbo right in his path. He desperately tried to get his plane to take off before he hit the massive airliner in front. The KLM's nose lifted steeply while its tail end slammed into the runway and scraped along the ground. But it was too late: the KLM jumbo smashed into the other jumbo, resulting in the deaths of 583 people. Miraculously, more than 50 survived.[43] It was, and remains, the world's worst aviation accident.

So the accident had happened not in the air, but on the ground. The jets had collided on the runway at Los Rodeos airport on Tenerife Island, Spain. The KLM aircraft, called the *Rhine River*, had brought passengers from Amsterdam. The other jet belonged to the now-defunct airline Pan Am, and carried passengers on a long-haul flight from Los Angeles via New York City. The Pan Am aircraft wasn't just any old 747; it was the *Clipper Victor*, the first-ever 747 passenger jet.

What caused the horrific mix-up? To find out, let's look at events leading up to the crash. Both planes were initially destined for the tourist destination of Las Palmas on the nearby island of Gran Canaria. As the planes headed for Las Palmas, news came through that a terrorist bomb had gone off there. So the airport was shut down and the jumbos were diverted to Tenerife, about 25 minutes away.

The KLM and Pan Am flights would now obviously be late – they would have to go to Tenerife and wait there until Las Palmas reopened. Many other flights were also diverted to Tenerife, causing congestion at Los Rodeos airport. The airport had only one runway, and wasn't accustomed to handling so much traffic and such large aircraft.

Both 747s landed without incident at Tenerife. The captain of the KLM, Jacob van Zanten, decided to refuel his plane while they waited for Las Palmas to re-open. Van Zanten also permitted his passengers to disembark and go into the terminal building.

The Pan Am, captained by Victor Grubbs, was carrying mostly elderly retirees as passengers. They were already tired after the long-haul flight. Grubbs didn't allow them off the aircraft, probably because he wanted to be ready to depart at a moment's notice. But the Pan Am was parked behind the KLM, which meant that it could leave only after the KLM had finished refueling and had its passengers back on board.

After some time, the pilots were told that Las Palmas airport had reopened. But the KLM plane hadn't finished refueling. Although the Pan Am was all set to go, it had to wait because there wasn't enough room for it to maneuver around the KLM in front of it.

Finally, the KLM plane was ready to depart. Unfortunately by this time, thick fog and low clouds had descended on the runway, a common occurrence on the island. The pilots couldn't see each others' planes, and neither could the controller at the tower see what was going on. There was no ground radar and the runway's center lights were out of action. Everyone had to rely on radio communications. Van Zanten realized that if visibility reduced further, the runway would be shut. Before the engines were started he said to his colleague, "Hurry, or else it will close again completely."[44]

The KLM was told by the control tower to move onto the runway, get into position and await take-off clearance. The KLM duly complied. The Pan Am was told to follow the KLM onto the runway, move along and leave the runway at the third exit, there being four exits in total. This would leave the runway clear for the KLM's takeoff.

What happened next was a series of terrible misunderstandings. The Pan Am crew were confused about which exit to take and, worse, the exits were not numbered. So the Pan Am missed its exit and headed for the next one. This meant it was on the runway for longer than it should have been.

Meanwhile, the KLM had taken its position at the start of the runway. The co-pilot radioed the controller saying they were "at take-off." This was an ambiguous statement because it didn't say whether the KLM was taking off or it was ready for take-off. To clarify, the controller said, "Okay, standby for take-off, I will call you."

The controller had also asked the Pan Am to report once it had cleared the runway. Captain Grubbs responded that he was still on the runway. But at that exact same instant, the controller had told van Zanten "Okay, stand by for take-off, I will call you." Since both the controller and Captain Grubbs radioed at the same moment, this caused a distortion in the radio communication, called a heterodyne. This can happen because pilots share a common frequency so they can hear each other's conversations. Hence van Zanten didn't hear the Pam Am's report that they were still on the runway. Van Zanten also didn't hear the controller's response that the KLM should stand by for take-off.

Without warning and without explicit clearance from the controller, van Zanten started his take-off run. He was earlier given clearance to fly a certain route after take-off, but he had apparently mistaken this as clearance for take-off itself. And because visibility was poor, van Zanten couldn't see that the Pan Am plane was still on the runway.

Remember the controller couldn't see what was going on and didn't have ground radar. But he knew Grubbs had not yet reported that he had cleared the runway. So the controller again asked the Pan Am to let him know once the plane had left the runway. The Pan Am replied that it would do so. This exchange was heard in the KLM cockpit and obviously indicated that the Pan Am was still on the runway.

Nonetheless van Zanten had got going and both he and the co-pilot were now concentrating on the plane's controls. They had apparently not heard the most recent radio exchange between the controller and the Pan Am.

But the KLM's flight engineer had listened. As his giant aircraft lumbered down the runway, the alarmed engineer asked van Zanten, "Is he not clear, that Pan American?" Van Zanten replied emphatically and apparently annoyed, "Yes," asserting that the Pan Am had indeed cleared the runway. The flight engineer didn't question van Zanten any further.

The KLM continued roaring with the Pan Am right in its perilous path. Soon, Captain Grubbs spotted the KLM jumbo jet looming upon him. He yelled, "There he is … look at him! Goddamn, that [expletive deleted] is coming!" Grubbs frantically tried swerving his plane out of the way. Van Zanten also saw the Pan Am jumbo directly in front and desperately tried getting his plane to fly over it. The captains' efforts were futile. The KLM tore into the Pan Am and everyone on board the KLM died. Several people on the Pan Am, including Captain Grubbs and co-pilot Robert Bragg, survived.

To summarize, here is the sequence of events:

- ■ The KLM is told to go to the end of the runway, turn around, and await take-off clearance. The KLM does this.

- The Pan Am is told to follow the KLM onto the runway, and take a left turn at the third exit to leave the runway clear.
- There are four exits on the runway.
- The Pan Am doesn't take a left turn at the third exit, and heads for the next one.
- The KLM begins its take-off run, with the Pan Am still on the runway.
- The planes collide.

What, or who, caused the disaster? There's no single answer because a series of unfortunate events culminated in the accident:

- The planes wouldn't have been at Tenerife had a bomb not gone off at their original destination, Las Palmas.
- If fog and low cloud had not descended on the airport, visibility would have been clear.
- If Captain Victor Grubbs and the control tower hadn't spoken at the same instant, there would have been no heterodyne.
- If the KLM pilot had used clear, unambiguous language, everyone would have better understood what he was doing.

These were the major contributing factors. But the investigators focused on van Zanten. Why did he take off without clearance?

To answer this, we need to comprehend the pressures on van Zanten. Recall that his flight had already been delayed. KLM airline regulations – like most airline regulations – stated that pilots could not work beyond a certain number of hours. Van Zanten was conscious that if they were delayed for too long, they would be forced to sign off from work and stay on the ground. Also, the weather could get worse and this would eliminate whatever little chance there was of flying. All this would result in more trouble for the passengers and more cost to the airline. It's not difficult to see that these factors were almost certainly playing on van Zanten's mind.

There was one more thing: van Zanten spent a lot of time teaching other pilots to fly in the flight simulator. In a simulator, the instructor is also the controller and the problem could be that van Zanten wasn't used to taking instructions from a control tower. But why didn't van Zanten pay greater attention to his flight engineer, who clearly doubted whether the Pan Am had left the runway?

You'll need some information on van Zanten to answer that question. As captain, van Zanten was senior to everyone else in the cockpit. He was a highly experienced and first-class pilot; in fact, he was at the top of the management chain as a pilot and also headed flight safety. His photo adorned KLM adverts. In short, van Zanten occupied a high position in the airline and this presumably gave him a great deal of authority. That's not all: van Zanten had trained the co-pilot for his 747 certification.[45]

Now imagine the situation in the cockpit. The captain is frustrated and very impatient because of the delays. He's anxious to get off the ground as soon as possible. The lower-ranked flight engineer, on hearing the exchange between the control tower and the Pan Am, wonders whether the Pan Am has cleared the runway. If the co-pilot has a similar concern, he doesn't say so. The flight engineer questions his captain. The captain probably takes offence, because there's no way he would get the wheels rolling if he's uncertain about the Pan Am. Annoyed, he responds to the flight engineer's query with a brusque "Yes." The flight engineer backs down. Given his superior's high status, it's not difficult to see why.

It's in crunch situations like this one that deeply ingrained mindsets are revealed. Often, it's the briefest of moments in a series of events that can be the difference between catastrophe and dull but comforting routine.

What made the crucial difference in the decision-making process in the cockpit? Van Zanten was the boss of the plane, so he could force his decision through. This is not an accusation but a reflection of reality at that moment. Perhaps if he wasn't under so much time pressure, he would have taken his flight engineer's concern into account and stopped the plane. But he felt pressured for time and ignored his flight engineer's doubt. Tragically, circumstances conspired in such a way that the dictator in van Zanten erupted.

As I've mentioned before, this eruption doesn't have to be an eruption of fury or anger. In the KLM cockpit, that eruption was a simple and forceful "Yes." On the flight engineer's part, there was an eruption of subject behavior – he kept quiet after pretty much being told to shut up.

Ultimately, although the investigators said there were mitigating factors, they pinned the blame on van Zanten because he had tried to take off without clearance. In other words, human error.

NASA, the US space agency, conducted a workshop on airline safety in 1979, in which it presented research that showed the vast majority of aviation accidents were due to human error. Specifically, these errors were in the areas of leadership, interpersonal communications and decision making.

As with most investigations of this kind, you always get told it's the big word issues like leadership or communication. You never get a direct statement like, "The boss threw his weight around, the subordinate got scared and so kept quiet." It's far too childish. You always get the grown-up version. It's the emperor's new clothes story again: you cannot talk about bosses.

Anyway, from NASA's workshop arose something called Cockpit Resource Management (CRM). The aim of CRM is to improve teamwork and communication in the cockpit by getting people to change their behaviors through training. Because of the already low accident rates in the airline industry and the fact that training is not standardized, it is difficult to tell whether CRM has improved safety.[46] Having said that, it's a step in the right direction because it at least recognizes the damage hierarchies can cause.

CRM has since been broadened to Crew Resource Management because all employees – not just crews in cockpits – are impacted by these behaviors. Regardless, CRM is considered another attempt at changing behavior through training. Some pilots have dismissed these efforts as "charm school" attempts at manipulating their personalities or just plain "psychobabble."

The other problem with CRM training is that pilots slip into old behaviors despite refresher courses.[47] But this is the problem with all kinds of training. CRM is meant to improve teamwork, but if training is the solution, then it won't be a long-lasting one.

And although CRM arose from a NASA workshop, NASA itself has suffered terribly from hierarchy. The tragic disasters of Space Shuttles *Challenger* and *Columbia* provide a graphic and awful demonstration of this, showing that wallpapering over the faultlines of the boss–subordinate power equation doesn't work.

# 13

# SPACE SHUTTLE
# *CHALLENGER*
# DISINTEGRATES

On a freezing morning in January 1986, *Challenger* blasted off
from the Kennedy Space Center in Florida. The shuttle mission
was all the more exciting because it carried Christa McAuliffe,
who was to be the first schoolteacher in space. But more than
excitement, one person on the ground felt great relief: As the
shuttle lifted off the launch pad and zoomed into the sky, a
rocket engineer said to his colleague, "We've just dodged a
bullet."[48] He evidently spoke too soon because 73 seconds into
its flight, *Challenger* disintegrated.

The astronauts may not have died straightaway. The crew
cabin continued to hurtle upwards before its ascent was halted
by the inexorable pull of gravity. Over two minutes after the
shuttle disintegrated, the crew cabin hit the Atlantic Ocean,
killing the seven astronauts on board. There's no telling if the
astronauts were conscious for the duration of the long drop
down. The only saving grace was they were perhaps rendered
unconscious by a lack of oxygen.[49]

What went so terribly wrong? Investigators found that a
problem with something called an "O-ring" (a kind of seal) had
caused the destruction of one of the two rocket boosters, on

which the shuttle rides. That was the technical reason. There was a people reason too. It turned out that engineers had pointed out the O-ring problem before the shuttle's launch, but they had been overruled by their bosses.

One of those engineers, Roger Boisjoly, had expected the shuttle to explode on the launch pad itself; hence his comment that they had "dodged a bullet" when *Challenger* lifted off, apparently safely. Boisjoly was the top O-ring expert at Morton Thiokol, the contractor that made solid rocket boosters for the shuttle.[50] A few months before the launch, Boisjoly had written a memo about the strong possibility of O-ring failure, explicitly warning management of the danger of "a catastrophe of the highest order – loss of human life."[51]

On the night before the launch, a teleconference was held between Thiokol and NASA. Because the forecasted freezing weather could severely impair the O-ring seal's performance, Boisjoly and other engineers had "fought like hell" to postpone the launch.[52] Boisjoly said, "There was never one comment in favor of launching by any engineer or other non-management person in the room."[53]

Lest you think all engineers are good and all managers are bad, note that several managers both at Thiokol and NASA were engineers themselves. Since they were managers, they had other pressures to deal with. NASA's bosses had to contend with the fact that several earlier launches had already been postponed. President Ronald Reagan's State of the Union address was coming up and if schoolteacher Christa McAuliffe was in space by then, the President was likely to give her a mention. NASA almost certainly wanted the shuttle up in time for the presidential address.

Further, NASA also had some unexpected competition from the European Space Agency. To prove that it gave value for money, the shuttle would have to fly often on an ambitious schedule.[54] Moreover, the cold war was still on during the 1980s, and the air force was arguing that NASA funds could be better used.[55]

For Thiokol, big money was at stake. The company and NASA were in the early stages of negotiating a contract worth $1 billion. This almost certainly put pressure on the Thiokol managers. Indeed, the Presidential Commission that investigated the disaster concluded, "[T]he Thiokol Management reversed its position and recommended the launch ... at the urging of Marshall [NASA] and contrary to the views of its engineers in order to accommodate a major customer."[56]

The problem was compounded because the engineers who recommended against launching didn't have the data to conclusively prove their case. The O-ring is made from a type of rubbery material, and hence at very low temperatures the material could freeze. This means the O-ring could become inflexible and not seal a gap as it was meant to, allowing hot gases to escape. However, the engineers couldn't prove the seal would fail in the freezing cold of launch day. But they knew it was a high-risk and potentially catastrophic operation and didn't want to take a chance.

The situation was a bit like the scenario in which automobile engineers have evidence that a car hitting a wall at say, 20 mph, gets damaged. They can guess that at 90 mph a crash could be fatal, even though they may not have the evidence to prove it. *Challenger* engineers were in a similar situation, so they recommended against launching.

In contrast to the "don't risk it" attitude of the engineers, NASA managers apparently wanted the engineers to prove that there was a risk. According to the Presidential Commission, "In this situation, NASA appeared to be requiring a contractor to prove that it was not safe to launch, rather than proving it was safe."[57]

Thiokol's engineering vice president was Bob Lund, and he initially supported his engineers' recommendation to postpone the launch. So did another Thiokol executive, Joe Kilminster. In response to their "don't launch" recommendation, Larry Mulloy, NASA's solid rocket booster program manager, said

"My God, Thiokol, when do you want us to launch, next April?" George Hardy, NASA's deputy director of science and engineering, said he was "appalled."[58] NASA challenged Kilminster and his engineers to prove from the existing data that it was unsafe to launch, which they couldn't do. While NASA didn't overrule Thiokol, there was clearly a stalemate. What do you think happened next?

Kilminster asked for some time to take their internal conversation offline. Jerald Mason, a senior executive at Thiokol, then told Lund to "take off your engineering hat and put on your management hat."[59] What does someone mean when he says that? It means: Take a status-based decision, not a facts-based one. Indeed, William Rogers, the chairman of the Presidential Commission, asked Mason, "[W]hen you spoke to Mr. Lund and told him in effect to take off his engineering hat and put on his management hat, wasn't that pressure on your part to a subordinate that he should change his mind?"[60]

Lund had dutifully changed his mind. So chairman Rogers asked Lund, "How do you explain the fact that you seemed to change your mind when you changed your hat?"[61]

The fact can be explained because Lund went from being a peer – when he agreed with his engineers – to being a dictator at the mercy of a more powerful dictator (his own boss).

At their offline conversation, despite the engineers' objections, the Thiokol bosses decided to go ahead with the launch. Boisjoly revealed:

> Some discussion had started between only the executives when Arnie Thompson [another engineer] moved from his position down the table to a position in front of the executives and once again, tried to explain our position. Arnie stopped when he saw the unfriendly look in Mason's eyes and also realized that no one was listening to him. I, too, received the some cold stares as Arnie, with looks as

if to say, "Go away and don't bother us with the facts." No one in management wanted to discuss the facts; they just would not respond verbally to either Arnie or me.[62] [W]hen he realized he wasn't getting through, he just stopped. I also stopped when it was apparent that I couldn't get anybody to listen.[63]

Another engineer, Brian Russell, testified that he wondered whether he was scared to speak his mind at the meeting: "I remember distinctly at the time whether I would have the courage, if asked, to stand up and say no."[64] When does the issue of courage come up? When there's another emotion involved: fear. But "luckily" for him, Russell's courage wasn't tested, since, "[W]e were not asked as the engineering people. It was a management decision at the vice president's level." Although his courage wasn't tested, Russell couldn't sleep that night: "I was nervous. You asked how I slept that night, and I said I thought I slept okay, and my wife differed with that."[65]

The managers' recommendation to launch was accepted by NASA without any further questions, because they had evidently got the answer they wanted.[66]

Note that in the corporate hierarchy, Boisjoly and Arnie (Arnold) Thompson were three levels below Kilminster and Lund, and four levels below Mason. Mason himself was three levels below the CEO.[67] It's not that these engineers were, to use Jack Welch's term, "boss haters." They were keenly aware of the pressures on their own employers and on NASA.

In his testimony, Boisjoly stated, "I felt personally that management was under a lot of pressure to launch and that they made a very tough decision, but I didn't agree with it."[68] Thompson testified:

> I also heard that Marshall's reaction was that they were appalled at our recommendation, and I was

very much surprised by this, having had the experiences over the years of how careful and conservative these people are, and I really admire them. And so I was extremely surprised.[69]

When Boisjoly got home after the teleconference, his wife saw the tension on his face and asked him the reason for it. He said, "We just were in a meeting where they made the decision to launch *Challenger* tomorrow and kill the astronauts. But outside of that, everything was great. It was a great day."[70]

Shouldn't Boisjoly have aired his objections vociferously, even if this meant risking his job? Recognize that if he was fired, at his age, 48, it would perhaps be difficult for him to get another job in his rarefied field of work. Unfortunately, Boisjoly's worst fears materialized – he was demoted and felt forced to leave because of the hostility of his employers. Not surprisingly, his health suffered and he struggled to find work after that. The aerospace industry, in which he had worked for over 25 years, shut him out. He said, "I couldn't get a job if I worked for free."[71]

Boisjoly's employer's response was the standard dictatorship response: instead of eliminating the problem, the dictatorship "eliminated" the person who raised the problem. It was classic "shoot the messenger." Dictatorships know that eliminating someone is the best way to silence everyone else. As Boisjoly said, "People are reticent to do that [stand up] because when they do, they get creamed, and that effectively silences others."[72]

In contrast, you would assume that everyone involved with missions involving human beings would be clearly told to shout out the bad news. But this doesn't happen because the organization structure allows only one kind of news to travel upwards: good news. As with Boisjoly, the system gets rid of bad news mercilessly: it eliminates the messenger.

In fact, one study of middle managers found a positive correlation between upward mobility and not telling the boss about things that had gone wrong. The most successful executives tended to hide information about problems.[73]

Since bad news is bad for its bearer, it morphs into good news as it moves up the organization hierarchy. The late Nobel prize-winning physicist, Dr Richard Feynman, served on the Presidential Commission that investigated *Challenger*. He noted that a one in 100 failure risk as assessed by engineers became a one in 100,000 failure risk by the time it reached top management. Feynman noted:

> [W]hy do we find such an enormous disparity between the management estimate and the judgment of the engineers? It would appear that, for whatever purpose, be it for internal or external consumption, the management of NASA exaggerates the reliability of its product, to the point of fantasy.[74]

Blaming management is a natural reaction, and that's what Boisjoly did. He took Thiokol to court for deceiving NASA, but lost. The court ruled that since no information was concealed, the issue was not deception but the interpretation of information. Managers just happened to interpret the information differently from the engineers.[75]

If no individual was at fault, what was the problem then? "Groupthink," a phenomenon researched by psychologist Irving Janis, was blamed. Groupthink is an occurrence in which a group of people, however smart, ends up making poor decisions by disregarding facts, just to maintain consensus.

Two personnel experts who conducted management seminars at NASA said groupthink was part of NASA's culture. Larry Mulloy, NASA's rocket booster project manager at the time of the *Challenger* disaster later admitted, "We at NASA got into a groupthink about this [O-ring] problem."[76]

But the engineers themselves had recommended against

launching, so how did they become part of groupthink? Isn't it strange that groupthink usually results in group members thinking what the bosses want them to think? Lawrence Wear, a NASA engineer, said that: "Everyone does not feel free to go around and babble opinions all the time to higher management." Further, he admitted that definite statements from (Marshall Space Flight Center) officials could have intimidated dissenters: "When the boss had spoken, they might quiet down."[77]

We could perhaps excuse non-engineer managers for not being sufficiently knowledgeable and hence rendered voiceless. But what caused the engineer managers to disregard the opinion of their own engineers? Simple: once they became bosses, they behaved as dictators. Obviously, they didn't suddenly become monstrous tyrants. The transformation was far more subtle: because they were their engineers' superiors, managers valued their own opinions more. In short, the bosses confused expertise with status.

Dictatorships are full of status-driven groupthink, because not thinking in tune with the bosses can be fatal. In a regular dictatorship, you could lose your life. At the workplace, you could lose your job.

As you can see, the *Challenger* episode was another example of an eruption of dictator behavior. No one was grossly abused. But subordinates were overruled and the prime dissenter eliminated. In any case, NASA took many measures, including emphasizing a culture of safety, to improve. Yet sadly, space shuttle *Columbia* didn't make it back home.

# 14

# *COLUMBIA* BREAKS APART

On January 16, 2003, space shuttle *Columbia* smoothly lifted off the launch pad. As you probably know, the shuttle doesn't lift off on its own. It's attached to an external fuel tank, along with the two solid rocket boosters. The external tank contains super-cooled – hundreds of degrees below freezing – liquefied gases and is covered with an inch-thick layer of insulating foam. The foam does two things. First, it prevents the gases in the tank from boiling. Second, it prevents ice from forming on the tank, since the ice can break off during launch and damage the shuttle. The foam is so effective that the tank's surface feels only slightly cool to the touch.

Exactly 81.9 seconds after lift-off on launch day, a piece of the insulating foam smashed into the shuttle's left wing after breaking away from the external tank. Actually, it was the shuttle that ran into the foam. This was because when the foam came off, it didn't immediately start falling downwards. Since it had been attached to the external tank that was shooting skywards at over 1,500 mph, the foam also continued upwards. But since it lost momentum after breaking off, it slowed down to 1,022 mph. The shuttle, attached to the external tank and rocketing up as fast, crashed into the foam at a relative velocity of about 545mph.[78] Nonetheless, the foam strike didn't seem to affect the shuttle because it reached its orbit as planned.

The shuttle's mission lasted 16 days and met all its objectives. With their work completed, the crew began their journey home on February 1. As the shuttle re-entered the earth's atmosphere, a NASA engineer on the ground, Rodney Rocha, monitored some of the shuttle's sensor readings. While he would normally watch the landing on NASA TV, he particularly wanted to keep an eye on the readings that day.

Managers had already starting thinking about future missions, but Rocha wasn't done with this mission just yet. Although *Columbia* was barely 16 minutes away from home, he had feared something could go badly wrong – and watched in horror as the alarm readings mounted. He said, "I started getting the sick feeling." He called his wife and told her, "I want you to say some prayers for us right now. Things aren't good."[79]

*Columbia*'s left wing was being melted by superheated air that had entered a hole created by the foam strike. Pieces of the shuttle were already falling off as it flew over the California coast. As the shuttle continued towards its landing site in Florida, aerodynamic forces ripped it apart over Texas. All astronauts on board died; the disaster later claimed two more lives when a helicopter crashed while searching for shuttle debris. *Columbia* wasn't just any old shuttle; it had been the first shuttle in space, way back in 1981.

After *Columbia* had launched, video footage showed the foam strike, but not very clearly. Since the engineers naturally wanted to find out the extent of the damage, they needed better images of the shuttle. While there was no guarantee that the astronauts could be rescued if the damage was severe, an attempt could perhaps be made, and at the very least, the extent of the problem would be known.

The Columbia Accident Investigation Board (CAIB) was the official body that investigated the disaster. According to the CAIB report, NASA's own ability to get images of shuttles during and after lift-off had worsened over the years as a result of budget and camera-team staff cuts.[80] NASA would now have to depend on the US military or other agencies for photos, through powerful ground telescopes or spy satellites.

The engineers were so concerned that they worked through the holiday weekend following the launch to analyze the foam strike. Although they had a mathematical prediction tool that could tell them how much the damage was, they couldn't be sure, and they didn't want to take a chance. So they wanted higher managers to request the photos they needed.

Rocha emailed a manager asking that the astronauts take a look at the area of impact, but didn't receive a reply. The problem was that high-level managers weren't as worried as the engineers. Even before the analysis had started, they believed the foam strike wasn't dangerous and that there was no need for a review over the weekend.[81] Several earlier shuttle missions had suffered from foam strikes without downing the shuttle, so one more strike appeared normal and routine.

At a meeting the following week, the chair of the Mission Management Team, Linda Ham, was updated about the foam strike. In response she said, "And really, I don't think there is much we can do, so you know it's not really a factor during the flight cause [sic] there isn't much we can do about it."[82] In short, she had already decided that nothing could be done.

To look into the foam strike, a team called the Debris Assessment Team (DAT) comprising of NASA and its contractor engineers had been formed. The DAT was co-headed by Rocha, himself an engineering chief. He was assigned with the task of formally asking for photos of the shuttle.

In an email to a manager, Rocha wrote:

> [W]e will always have big uncertainties until we get definitive, better, clearer photos of the wing and body underside. Without better images it will be very difficult to even bound the problem. ... Their

> answers may have a wide spread ranging from
> acceptable to not-acceptable to horrible, and no
> way to reduce uncertainty. Can we petition (beg)
> for outside agency assistance?[83]

A couple of other engineers were also trying to get the images, though outside the official chain of command, from the Department of Defense, which then started working on their requests.

Ham cancelled these requests;[84] moreover other managers stated there was "no need for the Air Force to take a look at the vehicle."[85] Astonishingly, the managers didn't even know much about the imagery facilities available to them. According to the CAIB, "[M]embers of the Mission Management Team were making critical decisions about imagery capabilities based on little or no knowledge."[86]

Appalled at the refusal by managers to ask for photos, Rocha asked an engineering manager for the reason. The manager said, "I'm not going to be Chicken Little about this," implying that he would not go around hysterically proclaiming the end of the world. Rocha shouted back, "Chicken Little? The program is acting like an ostrich with its head in the sand."[87]

Rocha had also drafted an email saying:

> In my humble technical opinion this is the wrong
> (and bordering on irresponsible) answer from the
> SSP [space shuttle program], not to request addi-
> tional imaging help from any outside source. I must
> emphasize (again) that severe enough damage ...
> could present potentially grave hazards. Remember
> the NASA safety posters everywhere around stat-
> ing, "If it's not safe, say so"? Yes, it's that serious.[88]

Rocha didn't send the email, but instead printed it out and showed it to a colleague. When asked why he didn't send the email, he said he didn't want to jump the chain of command,

and wanted to defer to management's judgment.[89] Also, he later said that after being repeatedly rebuffed by management, he "lost the steam, the power drive to have a fight because I just wasn't being supported."[90]

Nine days into the shuttle mission, the Debris Assessment Team presented its findings to the mission managers at a meeting. Because their request for images had been denied, DAT members had even considered inserting a slide requesting images in their presentation. But they dropped the idea.[91]

Engineers were so worried about the foam strike that the CAIB report stated, "so many engineers crowded the briefing room that it was standing room only, with people lining the hallway."[92] The DAT engineers concluded that their analysis, based on the uncertain information they had, didn't show a safety-of-flight issue existed. Although they stressed the uncertainty, engineers present at the meeting believed that the managers, rather than worrying about the uncertainties in the analysis, focused on the conclusion that there was no safety issue.[93]

Amazingly, it wasn't that the managers were unaware of the peril. The CAIB reported, "[A]ll the key managers were asking the right question and admitting the danger. Yet, little follow through occurred."[94] In short, the managers didn't want to hear the bad news that the shuttle could be in serious trouble.

The initial presentation by the engineers had been shortened to fit an earlier meeting schedule, but even so it was 40 minutes long. When it was presented at the MMT meeting, discussion on the damage was cut down to just three minutes by the meeting's leader, who was in a hurry to get to the conclusion that there was no serious damage.[95] At the meeting, the chair of the MMT, Linda Ham, declared there was "no safety of flight [issue], and no issue for this mission. ... Nothing that we are going to do different."[96]

Rocha and other engineers didn't challenge her and kept quiet. Why? The reason was that they were afraid to speak up. Rocha recalled:

> I remember a pause, and her looking around the room, like, "It's OK to say something now." But no one did. That made me feel very uncomfortable because I felt we should have said something ... I just couldn't do it ... I was too low down here in the organization, and she is way up here.[97]

Further, Rocha said, engineers were often told not to send messages much higher than their own rung in the ladder.[98] What happened to Rocha was exactly what studies have found: subordinate status itself – not expertise – can make people defer to their superiors' judgment. So hierarchy reared its ugly head again: because the bosses had already decided what they wanted to do, engineers kept quiet.

But Rocha was still anxious and had trouble sleeping. According to Daniel Diggins, a *Columbia* investigator, "I think that what was gnawing away at him was that he didn't have enough engineering data to settle the question he had in his mind."[99]

One colleague said, "He [Rocha] started coming by my desk every day. He was trying to be proper and go through his management." But, "he was too nice about it, because he's a gentleman; he didn't get nasty about the problem."[100]

Predictably, management was rebuked for the *Columbia* disaster. The CAIB report said, "Perhaps most striking is the fact that management ... displayed no interest in understanding a problem and its implications."[101]

But let's now look at the pressure on NASA management. NASA's chief is appointed by the US government, meaning NASA can be subjected to political pressures. The CAIB reported that after the cold war ended, NASA was left without a competitor. No political gains could be made from the space program; NASA's budget was cut by over 40 percent in purchasing power during the 1990s.[102] NASA's workforce was slashed by 25 percent and there was a hiring freeze; new or younger people couldn't be employed.[103] NASA was even considering privatizing the space shuttle.[104]

NASA's head at the time of the *Columbia* disaster was Sean O' Keefe. When he took charge of the space agency, he had said he wasn't a "rocket scientist" and that his expertise was in running large government programs.[105] In other words, he was a bureaucrat. O'Keefe had warned the agency saying, "NASA's credibility with the Administration and the Congress for delivering on what is promised and the longer term implications that such credibility may have on the future of Human Space Flight hang in the balance."[106]

It wasn't just the Human Space Flight program that was at risk. NASA's very existence was at stake. The CAIB noted, "The White House and Congress had put the International Space Station Program, the Space Shuttle Program, and indeed NASA on probation."[107]

In addition, there was also a deadline by which NASA had to effectively prove itself, a date that NASA had "seemingly etched in stone" – February 19, 2004.[108] Although this was a year after *Columbia*'s launch and apparently unrelated to the disaster, the date was extremely significant to NASA. It was the date on which a shuttle mission would deliver a critical part of the International Space Station that would "core complete" the space station.

This was important not only for the program, but also politically because both Japan and Europe would be able to connect their lab modules to the space station. To stress the importance of the deadline, NASA had even distributed computer screensavers to managers, counting down the days, hours, minutes, and seconds.[109] If the deadline wasn't met, NASA risked losing government support.

The deadline had looked realistic when it was first approved, in 2001. The problem was that events gradually ate into the schedule; technical glitches had also grounded the entire shuttle fleet. Months before the *Columbia* disaster, in September

2002, it was clear to shuttle and space station managers that the schedule as planned couldn't be met. So they used "tricks" to regain schedule margins and compressed the launch dates, with the February 19, 2004 deadline unchanged.[110] This raised concerns with many in the program. One stated that the system was at an "uncomfortable point" and that "I don't know what Congress communicated to O'Keefe. I don't really understand the criticality of February 19th, that if we didn't make that date, did that mean the end of NASA?"[111]

In effect, NASA had a gun held to its head and was told: "Deliver, or else." Such intense pressure translated into the pressure of ensuring that the shuttle schedules did not slip.

The CAIB report said, "Most of the Shuttle Program's concerns about *Columbia*'s foam strike were not about the threat it might pose to the vehicle in orbit, but about the threat it might pose to the schedule."[112]

Despite the gap of over a decade, the similarity between the *Challenger* and *Columbia* investigations is astounding. Just like in *Challenger*'s case where engineers had to prove that it was unsafe to fly rather than the opposite, *Columbia*'s engineers suffered the same requirement from managers. The CAIB reported, "The engineers found themselves in the unusual position of having to prove that the situation was unsafe – a reversal of the usual requirement to prove that a situation is safe."[113]

With the metaphorical gun pointed at them, it's not surprising that NASA managers ignored the foam strike. As part of their investigation, the CAIB asked shuttle and space station upper managers whether there was undue pressure to meet the February 19 deadline. The managers said no. The same question was put to the workforce, who said yes. The CAIB noted the evidence supported the workforce's view.[114]

In fact, the CAIB also asserted that "Managers' claims that they didn't hear the engineers concerns were due in part to their not asking or listening."[115] Why didn't the managers listen or ask? Because when you're a dictator, you think you're always right. And how were managers able to disregard the engineers? Easy – they had power over the engineers. What power? The power to fire people if they didn't obey orders.

Hierarchy runs deep in our organizational blood. While engineers were desperate for photos of the shuttle and approaching anyone they could, managers were more concerned about something else: whether engineers were going through the proper chain of command. The CAIB found, "Managers asked, 'Who's requesting the photos?', instead of assessing the merits of the request. Management seemed more concerned about the staff following proper channels (even while they were themselves taking informal advice) than they were about the analysis."[116]

Moreover, the CAIB said that in the battle between the engineers and managers, the managers won: "[E]ngineers concerns about risk and safety were competing with – and were defeated by – management's belief that foam could not hurt the Orbiter [the shuttle] as well as the need to keep on schedule."[117]

How did the managers win? What tactics did they use? The CAIB stated that "Mission Management Team participants felt pressured to keep quiet unless discussion turned to their particular area of technological or system expertise and, even then, to be brief." Further, "Program Managers created huge barriers against dissenting opinions by stating preconceived conclusions."

Why did these things happen? The CAIB felt the problems were caused by a "cultural fence" between managers and workers: "The phone and email exchanges ... illustrate another symptom of the 'cultural fence' that impairs open communications between mission managers and working engineers."[118]

But more than a cultural fence, it is a power fence because what impairs open communications is fear. The real problem was the status-driven dictatorship culture, which permitted only one-way communication and enabled management pressures to be pushed down the chain.

NASA had made many changes after *Challenger*, including emphasizing a culture of safety. So why did *Columbia* also perish? *Columbia* perished because the system was still the same. As the CAIB report said, "[T]here are unfortunate similarities between the agency's performance and safety practices in both periods."[119]

The problem for *Columbia* wasn't the lack of a safety focus – the problem was that the safety people kept their mouths shut too. The CAIB noted, "The safety personnel ... were largely silent during the events leading up to the loss of *Columbia*. That silence was not merely a failure of safety, but a failure of the entire organization."[120]

It wasn't so much a failure of the organization, as a failure of the dictatorship system. But once you know it's a dictatorship system, you don't need to be told that it's going to fail. Failure surprises us only because we think our organization systems are free. The reality is they're not.

The CAIB report also makes the critical point that employees may not even be conscious of their behaviors: "Solving NASA's problems is not quite so easily achieved. People's actions are influenced by the organizations in which they work, shaping their choices in directions that even they may not realize."[121]

If you don't realize how your choices and actions are being influenced, what does this mean? It means only one thing: your behavior is being programmed by something outside of you.

And just in case you're wondering how NASA's "dictatorship system" allowed the facts to be so openly revealed, remember that NASA is owned by a system in which people vote for their leaders.

After *Columbia*, NASA has tried to become fairer, and it's not just lowly engineers who were shunted off. Of the top 15 shuttle managers, 11 were reassigned or have retired.[122] But shunting off people isn't the solution, because the new people are not going to be "leaders" but dictators again. When you're a dictator, you automatically think you're way smarter than anybody else and expect – or force – everyone to play along. So playing along is what subordinates end up doing, even if that means going to war.

# 15

# THE UNITED STATES
# WAGES WAR ON IRAQ

The President of the United States, George Bush, decided that he'd had enough of Saddam Hussein's cat and mouse game with the United Nations. In March 2003, he gave the order for his mighty military machine to get rid of Saddam.

Saddam stood no chance, of course. He had counted on being able to withstand the US onslaught long enough for the international community to intervene. He wondered why his forces capitulated so easily. Saddam had been very confident about his own judgment because he was proved right in the earlier 1990 war – coalition forces had withdrawn without overthrowing him. His military had told him that they had sufficient firepower this time round to hold off the Americans until other countries asked the United States to back off. Moreover, his top officers also agreed with his battle plan and didn't challenge his assertions, which were based on the previous war.

As you know, the war didn't go according to Saddam's plan. It's not commonly known, but Saddam was a bit of a management theorist. He considered himself the CEO of a well-run, if ruthless, business. He wanted to know what had happened in organization terms. How did they so badly miscalculate their own strength and the Americans' resolve? For all his flaws, Saddam liked learning from his mistakes – he felt he needed to make a course correction soon to avoid being unceremoniously dethroned.

Saddam put his sons onto the job (this is before they died in the war). Humbled in the face of overwhelming defeat, his sons called in expensive Western-educated consultants to find out what had gone wrong. These consultants secretly conducted an investigation and drew several conclusions:

- The assessments made by senior officers reporting directly to Saddam overstated their military strength. These exaggerated reports were not supported by the underlying information provided by the officers on the ground.
- There was a "layering effect" such that as the reports moved up the ladder, they changed to reflect what Saddam really felt, rather than reality. Saddam's officers all knew that he didn't see the need to surrender.
- Everyone in Saddam's Mukhabarat Secret Service collectively agreed with Saddam's assessments, even though many of them were getting information to the contrary. (In other words, "groupthink.")
- Although it was too late, Saddam's sons realized that the problem really stemmed from a "broken corporate culture" in which the right information wasn't being passed along.

What would you have said to Saddam's sons? That if they had just paid you the money instead, you'd have saved them a lot of time and energy because these conclusions are blindingly obvious to anyone who's lived in a free system. In a dictatorship, subordinates are hardly going to disagree with the dictator. No wonder the intelligence reports were distorted as they moved up the chain. No wonder there was groupthink.

There's just one problem with this story. I've made it up. Saddam did apparently miscalculate his strength and he did apparently underestimate the resolve of the Americans. But while the "investigation" conducted by Saddam's sons is imaginary, the conclusions are real enough – only they're the conclusions drawn by the US Senate investigating the failure of the pre-war US intelligence assessments on Iraq.

Whatever your views on the rightness or wrongness of the war, let's look at the facts and the events leading up to the war without getting into a political debate. Why launch a war on Iraq even though Saddam was behaving like a deranged and dangerous pest? The stated official reason was that Saddam had weapons of mass destruction (WMD), and was therefore a threat to US and international security.

As far as the issue of WMDs was concerned, what should have happened compared with what actually happened? What should have happened is this. The US President asks his intelligence services whether Saddam has WMDs. According to the CIA, they then give the President the "best, unbiased and unvarnished information – regardless of whether analytic judgments conform to US policy."[123]

What actually happened? In the run up to the war, the CIA director at the time, George Tenet, had said there was a "slam dunk" case that Saddam had WMDs. (The term "slam dunk" comes from the game of basketball, implying a sure and easy thing.) After the war was fought and Saddam overthrown, exhaustive searches found no WMDs. With all the sophisticated and hi-tech intelligence gathering mechanisms at their disposal, how did the apparently omniscient US spooks not spot this?

Actually, they did spot it. They knew the evidence was weak, and that meant a war couldn't be waged against Saddam on the basis that he had WMDs. Nonetheless, Tenet declared that the Iraqi dictator definitely possessed WMDs.

The lack of WMDs was obviously a major issue because the case for war rested on the existence of those weapons. So the US Senate investigated the pre-war intelligence assessments to find out what had gone wrong. Following its inquiries, the Senate Committee reported its conclusions:[124]

- "Most of the major key judgments ... either overstated, or were not supported by, the underlying intelligence reporting." (Conclusion 1)

- "The Intelligence Community (IC) suffered from a collective presumption that Iraq had an active and growing weapons of mass destruction (WMD) program. This 'group think' dynamic led Intelligence Community analysts, collectors and managers to both interpret ambiguous evidence as conclusively indicative of a WMD program as well as ignore or minimize evidence that Iraq did not have active and expanding weapons of mass destruction programs. This presumption was so strong that formalized IC mechanisms established to challenge assumptions and group think were not utilized." (Conclusion 3)

- "In a few significant instances, the analysis ... suffers from a 'layering' effect whereby assessments were built based on previous judgments without carrying forward the uncertainties of the underlying judgments." (Conclusion 4)

- "Intelligence Community managers throughout their leadership chains ... did not encourage analysts to challenge their assumptions, fully consider alternative arguments, accurately characterize the intelligence reporting or counsel analysts who lost their objectivity." (Conclusion 5)

- "Most, if not all, of these problems stem from a broken corporate culture and poor management, and will not be solved by additional funding and personnel." (Conclusion 6)

The question is, why did Tenet and the other intelligence bodies give overstated opinions? How did they end up giving inaccurate information to the US President? And it wasn't just inaccurate information: according to Colin Powell, former US Secretary of State, the information was "in some cases, deliberately misleading."[125] This is absolutely astonishing. Getting things wrong is understandable. But why would the intelligence agencies present deliberately misleading information to their very own Secretary of State?

The reason is that years before the war, even before it came to power, the Bush administration wanted regime change in Iraq. Several members of President Bush's inner circle are part of an organization called the Project for the New American Century (PNAC). Before Bush became President, they had written to the then US President, Bill Clinton, asking that he have a strategy that "[S]hould aim, above all, at the removal of Saddam Hussein's regime from power."[126]

Since the name of the game was regime change, the intelligence chiefs only told the US President what he wanted to hear. But the Senate Committee said there was no evidence that the intelligence community was subject to political pressure.[127] Well, pressure doesn't have to be applied overtly at all. It doesn't take documentary evidence for subordinates to know what their bosses want. The Senate report goes on to say that "[T]he Intelligence Community had a tendency to accept information which supported the presumption that Iraq had active and expanded WMD programs more readily than information which contradicted it."[128]

Why would the intelligence folks do this? Just like in the case of the shuttle disasters, they ultimately fell in line with what their customer wanted. But the problem here was that the President was given wrong information. The intelligence agencies' job is to give the President information as they see it, not as the President may want them to see it. Why didn't this happen?

Let's answer this by elaborating on the Senate report's conclusions, starting with the first. "Most of the major key judgments ... either overstated, or were not supported by, the underlying intelligence reporting."

Who actually does the underlying intelligence reporting? It's definitely not done by robots, it's done by underling human beings. A senior military intelligence official said, "What I saw was that a lot of analysts, of low-level people, had it about right." But he added, "By the time you get to the executive summary level, it didn't look a lot like the analysts' views. And by the time you get to the unclassified public portion, all the mushiness and doubts were washed out."[129]

So who overstated the judgments? It had to be the underlings' bosses, all the way to the top.

Now consider the conclusion that "Intelligence Community managers throughout their leadership chains ... did not encourage analysts to challenge their assumptions, fully consider alternative arguments, accurately characterize the intelligence reporting or counsel analysts who lost their objectivity."

Why were the bosses doing this? They were doing this because there was top-down pressure to give the President the information and judgment he wanted. The fact that the "leadership chain" gets a mention means the Senate members had different expectations from these leaders. Leaders aren't supposed to behave the way they did. But flip the words "managers" and "leadership chain" to "dictators" and "dictatorship chain" and read that sentence again: "Intelligence Community dictators throughout their dictatorship chains ... did not encourage analysts to challenge their assumptions, fully consider alternative arguments, accurately characterize the intelligence reporting or counsel analysts who lost their objectivity."

Instantly, everything makes more sense. Dictators aren't the types to encourage questioning. The Senate members thought they were looking at one kind of animal – leaders – and they expected the relevant behavior. Instead, they found the behaviors of another animal – dictators.

Next, the report blames our old friend, groupthink. As in NASA's case, groupthink here meant the group had to think what the bosses wanted them to think: that despite the flimsy evidence, Saddam definitely had WMDs. The Vice-Chairman of the National Intelligence Council (NIC) said that he didn't believe that outside experts would have substantially different views and that, "I think all you could have called in is an amen chorus on this thing."[130]

From the Senate report, we know the intelligence agencies even had mechanisms to fight groupthink. It would appear that NASA's lessons had been learnt. But these anti-groupthink mechanisms weren't used. Why not? Because for these mechanisms to be used, the bosses have to agree for them to be used. It's not surprising the mechanisms were kept safely out of harm's way.

The report also blames the "layering effect" whereby assessments were built based on previous judgments without carrying forward the uncertainties of the underlying judgments. What does this really mean? That "bad" news at the bottom of the ladder turned into "good" news as it moved up the hierarchy. What was a shaky proposition at the bottom became a "slam dunk" certainty by the time it reached the President.

This is eerily similar to Richard Feynman's analysis of NASA – that as the risk (ie, uncertainty) assessments moved up the chain, the risks were so diluted that by the time the message reached the top, the risk factor was all but removed. If Feynman was alive, he'd probably say the same thing of the CIA that he did of NASA: that management exaggerated the reliability of its product (evidence of WMDs) to the point of fantasy ("slam dunk").

George Tenet, the CIA's chief, subsequently resigned and later regretted, "Those [slam dunk] were the two dumbest words I ever said."[131] Nonetheless, President Bush had awarded him with a Presidential Medal of Freedom, the country's highest civilian honor.[132] Spare a thought for the hapless Roger Boisjoly, ostracized for telling the truth about *Challenger*.

As in NASA's case, you're probably wondering how the CIA's "dictatorship culture" allowed the facts to be so openly revealed. Again, as in NASA's case, remember that the CIA is owned by a system in which people vote for their leaders. Imagine that – any person, from any country, belonging to any spy or other agency is able to view the US Senate report on America's intelligence failure on the Internet. In contrast, you wouldn't even put a tiny little cartoon of your boss on the company intranet.

It wasn't just the intelligence agencies that suffered from a dictatorship culture, the armed forces did too. General Tommy Franks headed Central Command (CENTCOM), the US military authority responsible for the Middle East and other regions; General Franks was hence also the man in charge of the Iraq war.

Franks frequently shouted or cursed at subordinates and one officer who worked closely with him said, "Central Command is two thousand indentured servants whose life is consumed by the whims of Tommy Franks. Staff officers are conditioned like Pavlovian dogs. You can only resist for so long. It's like a prisoner-of-war camp – after a while, you break."[133]

That wasn't the only problem: Franks's management style distorted the information coming up to him. The officer noted:

> I am convinced that much of the information that came out of Central Command is unreliable because he demands it instantly, so people pull it out of their hats. It's all SWAGS (Scientific Wild-Assed Guesses). Also, everything has to be good news stuff. ... You would find out you can't tell the truth.

At this point, let's revisit the organization chart from a systems perspective. You'll see clearly why truth telling goes out of the window. The layering effect will instantly make a lot more sense, because you now look at the chart as a bunch of boss and subordinate behaviors.

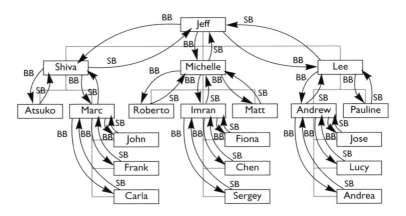

BB: boss behavior        SB: subordinate behavior

The Senate says the "layering effect" and other problems stem from a broken corporate culture and poor management, and cannot be solved by additional funding and personnel. Why not? Because the problem *is* the system.

The Iraq war and the *Challenger* mission had two very separate objectives, conducted by two very separate organizations, by people trained to do two very different things, with the two events being separated by a gap of almost 20 years. Yet, the investigations say exactly the same thing. Strange, isn't it? But it's not so strange when you consider that the organization systems were the same in both cases: dictatorship systems.

Of course, it's good that the investigations blame organizations rather than individuals, because it really is the organizations that are at fault. But the problem is that vague though important-sounding terms such as "organization failure," "layering effect," "broken corporate culture," or "groupthink" don't tell us exactly where the organization has broken down.

No one likes talking about exactly where the culture has broken down because it involves our bosses. We are only too aware that if we point this out, we could lose our jobs. Job insecurity is not a trifling matter because it affects our liveli-hoods, families, reputations, and even pensions. Why get into trouble by telling your boss about things that are going wrong, that he and his bosses don't want to hear about anyway?

You may think this happens only at the bottom rungs of the ladder. Powerful higher-ups don't get scared of their bosses. Or do they?

# 16

# EVEN GENERALS
# FEAR BOSSES

After Saddam Hussein's statue was toppled and he was caught hiding in a pokey hole, another major task lay ahead: reconstructing Iraq. Jay Garner, a retired three-star army general, was initially put in charge of this. His boss was the then US Defense Secretary, Donald Rumsfeld.

Garner had barely started work in Iraq when he was replaced by Paul "Jerry" Bremer, who would report directly to the President. Bremer disagreed with the way Garner was doing things and began making drastic changes straightaway. In his book *State of Denial*, the famous US journalist Bob Woodward described what happened next.[134] After Garner returned to the United States, he met Donald Rumsfeld and told him that Bremer had made "three tragic decisions": Disbanding the Iraqi army, banning Saddam's Ba'ath party members from government jobs, and dismissing interim Iraqi leaders.

Garner felt that with the Iraqi army disbanded, hundreds of thousands of Iraqi men would be left jobless, and these were men who still had weapons. They could turn against the Americans and create an intractable and vicious insurgency. Banning Ba'ath party members meant that they would go underground and cause trouble. Also, many professionals such as teachers, doctors, and engineers were required to be Ba'ath party members. By throwing them out, Bremer was eliminating the very people who could help get the country back on its feet. And by dismissing interim Iraqi leaders, Bremer was sending out the message that this was indeed an occupation by the Americans.

When Garner spoke to Rumsfeld about the mistakes, Rumsfeld didn't agree with his assessment. But Garner had at least told his boss the truth as he saw it. After his meeting with Rumsfeld, Garner met the US President, George Bush. Woodward wrote, "He [Garner] did not tell Bush about the three tragic mistakes he believed that Bremer, supported by Rumsfeld, had made. Once again the aura of the presidency had shut out the most important news – the bad news."[135]

Stop there for a moment and go through that again. A retired US three-star general is given the tremendous responsibility of putting a country back together after a devastating war. Yet, he doesn't tell the US President what he really feels about the way things are going.

Now really slow down and consider this: The US President is not just any old president and he's not just the leader of the world's only superpower. The US President has far more responsibility than that – he is considered the leader of the free world.

Step back and again review what happened because it's extremely important to fully grasp what's going on. The man responsible for reconstructing Iraq is not just any old American – he's a retired general from the world's most powerful armed forces. The US President is the leader of the free world. Put those facts together in a single sentence: An intelligent and brave man doesn't tell the leader of the free world what he really thinks.

Why should a free citizen be afraid of the leader of the free? "The aura of the presidency" perhaps. But common Americans routinely criticize and ridicule their President. Stand-up comedians poke fun at him. They don't seem to care about the aura. And here we have a former military man who's apparently become too tongue-tied to give bad news to the leader of the free. What on earth is going on?

Here's what is going on. When Garner saw the US President, he didn't see the leader of the free world. Garner wasn't a free citizen going to meet his leader. He wasn't in a country called the United States. He was in his workplace. When Garner saw the US President, he saw the commander-in-chief of the US military. He saw his boss's boss. He saw a dictator. How do we know this? Remember bearers of bad news in dictatorships are scared that they'll be gotten rid of.

Woodward asked Garner, "Do you wish now [over two years later] that you said, 'Mr President, as I just told the Secretary of Defense, in my view, I've been there and I need to make sure you understand what I think I understand. We've made three tragic mistakes.' Boom, boom, boom."[136]

Garner said he didn't know if he'd do that or not. But he added:

> I think if I had said that to the president in front of [Vice President] [Dick] Cheney and [Secretary of State] Condoleezza Rice and [Donald] Rumsfeld in there, the president would have looked at them and they would have rolled their eyes back and he would have thought, Boy, I wonder why we didn't get rid of this guy sooner?

Garner had already been replaced, and he was still worried about what his boss's boss would think. Garner wasn't the only one who kept his mouth shut. Woodward wrote:

> It was only one example of a visitor to the Oval Office not telling the President the whole story or the truth. The whole atmosphere too often resembled a royal court, with Cheney and Rice in attendance, some upbeat stories, exaggerated good news, and a good time had by all.[137]

To be fair, many underlings did question their superiors. But like in the sciences, if you have only one case that disproves the rule, you've got to worry about that case and the rule itself. You can't just wish it away or ignore it.

This is not very different from what was going on at Saddam's office before the invasion. Tariq Aziz, Saddam's deputy prime minister, was captured during the war. He said that no one could challenge Saddam's outdated war planning: "It was not allowed to raise your hand above anyone around you; it was dangerous. If a military leader disappeared, we do not know how it happened." An Iraqi air force officer, who until then was complaining about the loss of his force's capability, suddenly reported a 40 percent improvement. A captured general from Saddam's elite Republican Guard stated, "It was at this time that everyone started lying."[138]

Aziz also said he had opposed the invasion of Kuwait in 1990, but couldn't dissuade Saddam. When asked why he stayed on rather than resigning, Aziz responded that although he didn't fear for his life, "[T]here would be no income, no job."[139]

Aziz wasn't the only high-ranking official who backed down. Former vice president Taha Yasin Ramadan believed that from late 2002, Saddam's policy was putting Iraq on the path of a ruinous war with the US. But he said, "I couldn't convince Saddam that an attack was coming. I didn't try that hard."[140] Saddam's Minister of Military Industry, Al Mullah Huwaysh, said no minister ever argued in meetings against Saddam's stated position because it "was unforgivable. It would be suicide."[141]

Saddam's son, Qusay, was no better. A Republican Guard major general said, "He thought most of us were clowns. We pretended to have victory, and we never provided true information as it is here on planet earth. Qusay always thought he'd gain victory. Any commander who spoke the truth would lose his head."[142]

Obviously, Saddam was brutal with his subordinates in a way the US President would never be, but let's compare the end results. Underlings in the US President's administration don't speak up to him. Underlings in Saddam's regime don't speak up to him. What's the difference? There's no difference. There's no difference because there's no difference between the workplace system and the dictatorship system. You couldn't get a more spine-chilling example if you tried.

Let's now put the subplots together to see how events led inexorably to war:

- The US President wants Saddam knocked out because the Iraqi dictator apparently has WMDs.
- Although the CIA doesn't have substantial and compelling evidence, it tells the US President that Saddam definitely has WMDs (because of the "layering effect").
- Saddam's people either tell him he has WMDs or exaggerate their fighting capability (the layering effect again).
- Saddam says he doesn't have WMDs but leaves room for doubt; he behaves defiantly.
- From Saddam's behavior and US intelligence reports, the US President "knows" that Saddam definitely has WMDs.
- The US President orders his military to invade Iraq.

Think about it: The Iraq war was perhaps fought only because two sets of people were too scared to tell their bosses the truth. These two sets of people, belonging to two different nationalities, different religions, different cultures, and different ideologies, shared one thing in common: fear of the boss.

The war wasn't the only consequence of this fear. Saddam ended up being executed. President Bush's Republican party ended up getting a self-confessed "thumping" in subsequent elections.[143] And Iraq continues to struggle.

Fear is the defining attribute of a dictatorship system, and boss behavior can be the daily drip-drip water-torture occurrences in which bosses routinely and pettily harass subordinates. This is distressing enough in itself. But certain common factors seem to trigger dictatorial behavior, going beyond the harassment of subordinates. And these dictatorial eruptions can cause the deaths of people.

## Factors that contribute to a dictatorial "eruption"

Both bosses and subordinates are especially vulnerable to a "dictator eruption" and "subject eruption" when a situation has these factors:

- decision pressure: the need to make a decision
- ambiguity of information: no clear answers
- time pressure: the need for speed
- other pressures: such as financial and political pressures.

The four incidents – the Tenerife accident, the *Challenger* and *Columbia* tragedies, and the Iraq war – span a period of three decades. We can use these events and organizations as proxies for the prevailing boss–subordinate relationship in organizations over this lengthy time period. We can see that for all the talk of empowerment, self-management, and leadership, nothing has changed on the ground in all these years. And nothing has changed because the system is still the same.

As we've seen, power and status result can result in bouts of stupidity from otherwise extremely smart people. I call this phenomenon "Status Induced Stupidity" – SISY, pronounced sissy. (It had to come some time – my contribution to management jargon.)

Reflect now on Abraham Lincoln's remarkably perceptive words echoing down the centuries: "Nearly all men can stand adversity, but if you want to test a man's character, give him power."

Of course, SISY doesn't apply only to bosses; while bosses feel their superior status makes their knowledge "superior," subordinates feel their inferior status makes their knowledge "inferior." So subordinates can suffer from SISY too.

An experiment was conducted in which military pilots and navigators were asked to solve a logic problem. It turned out that the pilots were more likely to speak convincingly of their solution than their lower-ranked navigators. This happened even if the pilots were wrong and the navigators were right. And the navigators conceded to the pilots even if they hadn't met the pilots.[144]

We've seen how dictatorial systems can really mess up things. But is there a positive example, an example in which a free system won in the toughest of scenarios – a war? Yes, there is. It happens to be another war on Iraq, but Iraq wins this time. The enemy? The United States.

# 17

# THE UNITED STATES
# LOSES A WAR

Take on a really tough challenge. How about taking on the world's most powerful armed force in history? How would you like to take on the might of the United States with all its superbly trained soldiers, high-tech weaponry, nuclear-powered aircraft carriers, armed-to-the-teeth warships, thunderous fighter-jets, and stealth bombers?

Your instant response would be, you wouldn't. But if you wanted to think about it, you would first ask, what do I have my disposal? Well, you have just a handful of small boats, planes, and a bunch of rag-tag volunteer fighters.

Knowing this, would you now take on the challenge? If you're rational like most people, there's no way you would. No one in his right mind would want to take on the United States. It would be a hopeless cause and a foolish one at that. But a 64-year-old retired man took on the massive military might of the United States, and won.

If you haven't heard of this man, it's because although he defeated the US armed forces, he did it in a simulated exercise. If the battle happened in real life, he really would have won.

Just who is this man? He's an American himself. His name is Lieutenant General Paul Van Riper, a retired US marine. He took part in a massive war exercise called the Millennium

Challenge that was staged in 2002, well before the real war on Iraq. The simulated war was between two opposing forces – the Red force, headed by Van Riper, and the Blue force, which was the United States. The Red force was presumed to be a rogue Middle-Eastern country, resembling Iraq.

Millennium Challenge was the biggest war game of all time; it cost $250 million and involved a combination of live military exercises and computer simulations. Over 13,000 real troops took part. The purpose of the exercise was to test the US military's ability to conduct something called Rapid Decisive Operations (RDO).[145]

The exercise was planned for three weeks and it was assumed that it would be a no-contest, with Blue winning handsomely. But reality turned out rather differently: within the first few days, most of the expeditionary Blue fleet was on the ocean floor. Red routed Blue, leaving thousands of US soldiers "dead."

How did Van Riper achieve such an astonishing victory? He used a low-tech, unconventional approach that avoided the use of electronic equipment. Motorcycle riders passed on messages, and calls to prayers from mosques gave coded instructions to fighters. Suicide attacks were launched via small boats on the large US ships, and pilots didn't use the radio to communicate.

No doubt, these were important factors in his victory. But crucially, what was Van Riper's "leadership style"? In his own words, he said, "The first thing I told our staff is that we would be in command and out of control."[146] Van Riper only stated the intent of what needed to be done; his subordinates were told to take their own initiative and not depend on orders from the top.

Terrorist organizations operate in much the same way. The leadership provides a straightforward and clear intent such as: "kill the enemy." The "subordinates" on the ground then decide what needs to be done and then do it. Also, terrorist leaders inspire tremendous loyalty precisely because they are leaders – their "subordinates" have voluntarily accepted their leadership, so much so that they are willing to die for them.

Anyway, the Millennium Challenge story doesn't end there. After Red beat Blue hands down, the Blue navy was "refloated" so that all the previously sunken ships were back on the water. The dead soldiers came back to life and the exercise began again. Apparently, the military does this quite regularly – if there are a few days of an exercise left, it makes sense to use that time to try out other things. Otherwise, a lot of effort and money goes to waste.

So the war games restarted. A few days into the new game, Van Riper noticed his orders were being countermanded by his subordinate.[147] Instead of taking his orders from Van Riper, the subordinate began taking orders from someone else, a different boss. Who was this mysterious other boss? He was the subordinate's real-life boss. Whose team was the real-life boss on? The Blue force. Not only was the real-life boss a part of the Blue force, he was the director of the entire war exercise.

Van Riper said that from then on, the war games were scripted to a known, predefined conclusion, that of a Blue victory. Red duly lost.

Did Van Riper's subordinate do the right thing in the war game? Obviously not. Lest you look on with smug complacence, ask yourself: would you have disobeyed the commands of your real boss in the US military? Not so easy now, is it? Especially in the military, you do not disobey orders from your boss, even if those orders are crazy. "Don't question orders" is something that's drilled into soldiers. It's no wonder that small groups using guerrilla tactics frequently do massive damage to much larger forces. Without chains of command to go through, the guerrillas on the ground pretty much do what they want, when they want, and how they want.

And what does the term "chain of command" actually mean? It means only one thing: a chain of bosses, each increasingly distanced from the real action, all the way up. While a chain-of-command hierarchic structure looks very neat and clean, it simply cannot withstand the pressure of real-life battles, which are anything but neat and clean. Real life is complex. In systems language, it's a wicked problem. To attempt to deal with complexity with a tame solution is to invite disaster.

One of the more biting criticisms that Van Riper made of both the US civilian and military leadership was the use of excessive and meaningless jargon. In stark similarity to the jargon that business "leaders" are known to spew, Van Riper said:

> [W]hether the slogan is something like "information superiority" or "dominant manoeuvre" or "effects-based operations," these things just kind of fall out as assertions of what we want, and then ask people to write to them. There is no content, so consequently they can't write anything meaningful, but they're being asked, or in some cases being paid, to write, and they write, and they write. And it's terrible.[148]

That's exactly the problem with management jargon. It uses wonderful and important-sounding words like leadership, but it disguises real problems.

It's not that we're always unaware of this; we do have a sense that dictatorships and hierarchies are bad. Despite this, we persist with bosses because we think hierarchy is natural – that it is a product of nature. And since we can't fight nature, the apparent laws of nature have infiltrated into our offices.

# 18

# BOSSES USURP
# DARWIN

For all the progress we've made as human beings, we can't seem to get rid of the notion of superiority, inferiority, and the pecking order. Many argue that it's "natural" because that's how nature works. The truth is that nature works in exactly the opposite way. Hierarchy is an artificial construct. To justify hierarchy in nature, we often draw a food chain that has humans at the top and single-celled creatures at the bottom. We then state that because we're at the top and we can out-think and literally eat the animals and creatures below us, there's automatically a hierarchy.

Yet, how does nature really work? Let's say we order that all trees must be cut. The trees are cut. We're left with the land that we want. End of story. Nothing else is supposed to happen. But being a system, an obviously pesky and uncooperative one at that, nature hits back with climate change. If human beings were indeed top dogs in the natural scheme of things, global warming would not have happened, but it has.

In contrast, what's supposed to happen in a hierarchy? You act on something that's "inferior," and it stays acted upon. Nothing else is supposed to happen. There shouldn't be any feedback, or "back-talk" as scientific management expert Frederick Taylor would put it. You move a chair, and it stays moved. Nothing else happens.

The point is that human beings are part of nature's system too. Nature isn't hierarchical and hierarchy isn't "natural." If you disagree that nature is a system, note that we already have a word for nature's system: ecosystem.

Increasingly, several organizations today think of themselves as players in an ecosystem. They've got that part right – externally, they're parts of a system in which they live and function. Competitors, vendors, suppliers, investors, regulatory bodies, and customers are all parts of that system. Everyone has an impact on everyone else.

But unfortunately, what organizations haven't yet realized is that internally too, they are systems. The people who work there are parts of that system. The problem arises when something is really a system and we mistakenly think of it as a hierarchy.

Once we decide that organizations are hierarchical, we draw top-down organization charts to reflect that hierarchy. But this is to confuse hierarchy as a method of organization that helps us picturize our thoughts, with hierarchy as a method of command-and-control.

For example, to understand the working of the human body, we can visualize it like this:

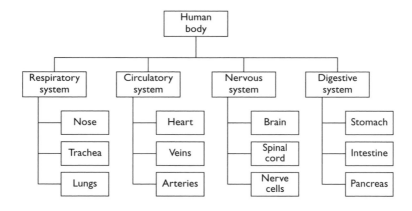

Although we can draw the human body system as a hierarchic structure to better understand it, this doesn't mean the body works in the same way. We know that. Unfortunately, what we do with organization charts is exactly the opposite. We turn what should be only a model or chart to help us organize our thoughts into a real-life command-and-control structure.

It isn't always wrong to have a map that doesn't reflect reality, if this indeed helps us. Take the map of London's underground "tube" commuter rail network. If you don't know how to get from one place to another, here's what you do. You pick up a little map of the tube network (also available online), and plan your journey. The interesting thing is that the map doesn't reflect actual distances, curves in the route, and so on. Instead, the map simply has the train stations at regular intervals, with the routes heading off at fixed angles.

You cannot use the map to judge exact distances or absolute positions of stations. If you tried using a tube map like a road map, you'd be very confused. You'd wonder why your train seems to be taking varying times to travel from station to station, when on the map all stations appear equidistant from each other. You'd wonder why your train is turning this way and that, when the map just shows a straight line.

So the tube map has no direct bearing on reality. But it is an excellent guide to help you get around the tube network. What would happen if you expected the tube map to reflect reality? You'd be trying to force reality to fit the map you have in front of you. But at the most, you'd be seriously confused. What happens when we try to force the map of the top-down organization chart onto human beings? People get seriously ill. As we saw earlier, people get serious diseases according to the grade they belong to. In effect, what's the human body telling us? That something is drastically wrong with the map we're using.

Allied to this hierarchical map, we enforce another "natural" phenomenon at work: the "survival of the fittest." Hierarchy and "survival of the fittest" are the twin pillars on which the edifice of the modern organization rests. Perhaps the most important unwritten rule at the corporate workplace is this: you've got to be tough. If you can't survive in the organization, you aren't tough enough, and therefore you've got to be thrown out. Let's look at the commonly known version of "survival of the fittest" in a little more detail.

## The fight to the death

Take our alpha male. He climbs to the top of his hierarchy by being the toughest and meanest baddie around. If any weakling male gets on the wrong side of the alpha male, he's in for a pounding or even death. Once our alpha reaches the top, what's his objective? His aim is to propagate his genes by mating with as many females as possible.

This is what we commonly know as the "survival of the fittest." The term "survival of the fittest" has been attributed to Charles Darwin as part of his theory of evolution, but it was actually coined by an English philosopher, Herbert Spencer. Darwin preferred to use the term "natural selection," though Darwin himself said that "survival of the fittest" was a more accurate term.[149]

What did Darwin mean when he said "survival of the fittest"? He didn't mean the survival of the biggest, the toughest, or the strongest. He meant those who could best adapt to their environment and survive – those "fit" *for their unique environment*. It's important to note that in Darwinian terms, survival is always inextricably bound to the environment in which an organism lives.

So survival is not an absolute such that survival means survival absolutely everywhere and under any circumstances. Thus, in the desert, camels are fit to survive. On mountains, we have mountain goats. In the sea, it's the fish and other salt-water creatures. You don't see a shark fighting a tiger on land. You don't see a polar bear fighting a camel in the desert. You don't see an elephant fighting a whale in the ocean. You don't see a giraffe fighting an eagle in the sky. That's because these animals have adapted to survive in their own environments. If you take an animal from its environment and put it in another one, it dies. The point is, the environment plays a massive role in determining who survives and who doesn't.

Moreover, "survival of the fittest" is an individual goal, not a team goal. Remember, this is the commonly known version of the notion of survival of the fittest. In actual fact, Darwin also took into account "altruistic" behavior – behavior in which an animal helps other animals, often at a cost to itself. Darwin noted that altruistic behavior takes place when animals are intelligent and social.[150]

Although human beings are intelligent and social, Darwin's theory of natural selection and "survival of the fittest" has nonetheless taken hold in our offices. Whether or not you believe Darwin, our organizations sure are believers. Hence, organizational mechanisms are set up in similar fashion. Many companies rate employees and then eliminate the bottom 10 percent – or some other arbitrary percentage – in which the "weaklings," "laggards," or "non-performers" are culled. When we say "companies rate employees," it goes without saying that the ratings are handed out by bosses. Dismissals, in a rather interesting coincidence, are called "firings" – the "killing" of a non-performing "not fit" individual.

Hence, individuals in companies feel compelled to behave competitively and aggressively as individuals. There's an understated savagery at our workplaces. We decide that because it's a Darwinian world, we need to survive and get to the top not only by performing well ourselves, but also by putting down competing colleagues through emotional violence, non-cooperation, backbiting, and any which way. Obviously, all this is done with extreme sophistication, extreme brutality, or anything in between.

From a company standpoint, usurping Darwin and putting him to work at our offices seems like a good thing. Because only those who survive and win internally are good enough for the company. But this logic becomes flawed when you take a subordinate's environment into account. The role of the environmental conditions in determining who survives is a critical distinction to make. Let's understand this through an imagined scenario, in which you're going to be an elite athlete.

# 19

# MANAGEMENT AS ENVIRONMENT

Say you want to represent your country in a sprint event in the forthcoming Olympics. Obviously, you're first going to have to go through a qualifying competition that pits you against your fellow athletes.

Because there are so many competitors, this is done in batches. Your batch is slotted for the last session of the day. But because of some unforeseen delays, it turns out that it's too late in the evening for your batch. The race is put off for the next day. You're also told the venue has been changed as the current venue has already been booked for another event.

The following day, you and your fellow competitors arrive at the new venue. You walk up to the track to examine it, and notice that it is filled with potholes. There are no lines to distinguish one lane from the next. There's no finishing tape at the other end, so you don't know exactly how much distance you have to cover.

Soon, dark clouds gather and it starts raining heavily. Large hailstones smash into the ground. A hurricane-force wind tears across the stadium. The track turns into a muddy slush and small pools form in the potholes. Visibility is reduced to almost nothing.

Obviously, the race will be called off. You head for shelter.

But no, the race official indicates that the competition will go ahead. All of you are stunned. The official says that those who don't take part will be out of the reckoning. Everyone protests but the official doesn't budge.

All of you reluctantly take to the starting line. The starter gun pops and the race is on. You don't know where you're headed because you can barely see. You keep bumping into the other athletes. Because the track is so slippery, you fall several times and hurt yourself. But despite the extreme conditions and your injuries, you urge yourself on. Finally, you see an official indicate that you've reached the finishing line.

The official announces the race times of all the competitors. Predictably, the times are poor. The race official says that no one has qualified because your race times are unacceptable at this elite level.

All of you crowd around the official and again complain about the race conditions. But the official shrugs his shoulders and says, "We are a strictly meritocratic organization. We accept no excuses. If you don't make the qualifying time, you're out. If you have any sense, you'll sit back and reflect – whether you lack motivation, talent, skill, or the right attitude."

Why does this story sound so preposterous? It sounds crazy because this doesn't happen in real life. Whenever there's an athletic competition, it's assumed the conditions are ideal. That the sun is shining, the track is fully prepared, the lanes are clearly marked, visibility is perfect, and so on. Months, sometimes years, are spent on preparing venues for high-level sport such as the Olympics. Everything is planned and executed so that the elite athletes are given the best possible environment in which to perform.

Why is so much effort spent on this? The reason is that, obviously, the conditions have a huge impact on an athlete's performance. The conditions never get a mention because it would be ludicrous to keep saying, "The athletes' times were achieved in ideal performance conditions." The conditions are always supposed to be ideal. Now, what do environmental conditions and athletic performance have to do with bosses?

All bosses have their own management style. They could be autocratic, consensus-driven, paternal, authoritarian, or whatever. This management style results in a "management environment" in which the subordinate has to perform.

Bosses may often scream or not say much at all. They may be approachable or send out strong vibes that shout "don't come anywhere near me." They may communicate clearly or be as enigmatic as the Mona Lisa. They may expect you to join in their drinking parties, or want you to stay well away from them outside office hours. They may want to micromanage you or prefer to not be there at all. All this forms part of the management environment.

Clearly, a subordinate's performance is greatly impacted by the management environment. Nonetheless, this is never taken into account when the subordinate's performance is assessed. It's not difficult to see why. Unlike nature's environment, the management environment isn't visible.

Worse, the person doing the assessment is the person who's creating the management environment in the first place. Imagine the weather judging the athlete's performance. The weather could be really nasty, and then give the athlete the lowest possible performance-rating, and blame it on the athlete. The athlete would then be deemed unfit to survive. It sounds insane, but what never happens on the racetrack happens all the time in our offices.

How else does this logic pan out at our workplaces? Well, the theory goes that those who survive are the best people for the jobs. But as we know only too well, this is most definitely not the case. Those who survive are those who best adapt themselves to the management environment created by their boss. In short, those who survive are not necessarily good for the company; but it's mandatory that they be good for their bosses.

It's not that survival of the fittest is a bad strategy. It works fine if you are trying to fight, survive, and win as an individual. But in the organizational context, if everyone is busy fighting, surviving, and trying to win as individuals, will the organization survive and win?

And if there's one thing that organizations talk about more than the "survival of the fittest," it's change. Darwin had noted, "It's not the strongest of the species that survives, nor the most intelligent, but the one most responsive to change." So we have change management, change agents, change experts, et al. Change is a big deal. But why do organizations have such a problem in being responsive to change?

## Change

It has to be said that as human beings, we mostly don't like change. But if we have to, there are two ways we "do" change: we drive change, or we actively resist it. What systems drive change? Conversely, what systems resist change?

As always, the best thing to do is look around to see what happens in the real world. It's obvious that free systems drive change and fear systems resist change. Free systems seem to be in a perpetual state of flux. Even if the people in free systems don't particularly like change, they go through it kicking and screaming.

In contrast, subjects in fear systems can't change or don't change because they're frozen with fear. For their part, dictators don't like change because it means a loss of control. They do everything in their power to ensure the status quo is maintained. And they are often spectacularly successful at this – many dictators enjoy long periods of unbroken rule. Fidel Castro of Cuba has been in power since 1959, and Saddam Hussein ruled for nearly a quarter of a century before being ousted by the United States. North Korea's Kim Il Sung ruled for 48 years until his death in 1994; his son took over and still rules. Libya's Colonel

Gaddafi has ruled since 1969 while Zimbabwe's Robert Mugabe has ruled since 1980.

The issue is not whether dictators are personally successful in holding on to power for long periods. The issue is: Are their countries changing for the better? Are their countries succeeding? Are they progressing, stagnating, or regressing? The reality is that in these countries, time stops. They are not responsive to change because there is no incentive to change – in fact, there are brutal disincentives to change. It's not surprising that there is little or no innovation. People are forever trying to survive, not thrive.

It's not just the dictator who resists change. Those lower down the hierarchy also have a vested interest in keeping the hierarchy alive, because that's from where they derive their power. So the hierarchy thrives while the country languishes or perhaps even self-destructs, like the former Soviet Union.

Now, if bosses are dictators, how have organizations in free systems driven change so far? Well, even if they don't drive change, more nimble and freer competitors thrust change upon them. If organization fear systems continue to resist change in the face of the changing demands of the marketplace, these organizations eventually die. More importantly, the wider environment in which they live – the free system – doesn't interfere. The free system simply sets the rules by which everyone has to play. Hence, companies have had to change and innovate to survive.

The lesson is clear: to survive and thrive, your organization must have the capacity not only to change, but to drive change. And the only way to build that capacity is to create a free system.

It's often said that the technological advances of the 20th century are greater than those of all the previous centuries put together. But it's no small coincidence that with more freedom, we've had more advances at a far greater pace than ever before.

We always wonder what the world will look like in future, what with unimaginable and fantastic advances. But have you ever wondered what kind of organization it would take to make those fantastic things happen? What will the organization of the future look like? The answer is pretty easy – it will be an organization that's willing to unlock the shackles that bind its employees and truly set them free.

Of course, organizations today are far more "free" and "flat" than they were during the height of the command-and-control era of the industrial age. Incremental improvements over a long period have meant that organizations have changed with changing times.

However, freedom is still not institutionalized. Moreover, even a "flat" organization with just two levels cannot be called truly flat, just as a flight of stairs with only two steps cannot be called flat.

Thus despite gradual improvements, the hierarchical command-and-control model is still with us. The report into the *Columbia* disaster noted, "Cultural norms tend to be fairly resilient. … The norms bounce back into shape after being stretched or bent."[151] What does this mean? It means that we can change and improve a caterpillar as much as we want, but we will still end up with a caterpillar. If we want to fly, we need to turn into that beautiful thing with wings: the butterfly. And to do that, we need a quantum leap in thinking.

# Section

# IV

## The Way Forward

# 20

# FROM CATERPILLAR
# TO BUTTERFLY

For organizations, the quantum leap of going from a crawler to a flyer means institutionalizing freedom. Instead of fear, we need to put freedom at the heart of the organization. And the surest way to do that is to give subordinates the right to vote for their leaders.

This is not to suggest that a free system is a neat and clean solution, a magic bullet that will solve all our problems. Remember that organization systems are wicked problems and these problems have no definitive solutions. Rather, we can only work towards making things better. That's why this section is called the "way forward" rather than the "solution." So the process of transitioning to a proper free system is going to be an evolving one.

Free countries continually evolve with changing times, and their legislative, executive, and judiciary frameworks have to keep pace with changes. "Solutions" continually throw up new issues, and once these are solved, they throw up newer ones. But fundamentally, things get better. And so it will be with our workplaces.

You may like the idea of a free system, but at the same time you may feel that giving subordinates the right to vote is downright bizarre. Several questions will arise:

- Is it the subordinates' place to choose their leader?
- Won't there be anarchy?
- What do subordinates know about leadership?
- Are subordinates intelligent enough to choose their leader?

And so on. But consider this: before women won the right to vote, this was exactly the view held of them – that they weren't intelligent enough, that they too emotional, hysterical, or knew nothing of politics or leadership. It was also the view held of African-Americans in the United States. There was a notion that everything would go haywire if those of a "different" gender or race were allowed to vote. And it's also the same excuses that today's dictators trot out – that their people are too stupid, ignorant, irresponsible, or just "not ready."

If we want true leadership, it's vital that we respect the intelligence of people, however ridiculous it may sound. Always keep in mind that the people are not assessing the leader's intelligence, technical expertise, or prowess. They're assessing the leader's ability to lead them. So Einstein's subordinate wouldn't be assessing Einstein's proficiency in physics, he'd be assessing Einstein's leadership of him.

Ultimately, what's the most important thing about having the right to vote? Is it about choice? Is simply being able to put a tick mark on a slip of paper next to your preferred man or woman? Is it the paraphernalia of voting – elections, speeches, campaigns, and so on? Yes, voting is about all these things. But there's something else that forms the bedrock of the vote. And that's the P word – power.

## Voting is about power

More than anything else, voting is about your power – your power over your leader. You can throw the person out if you want to. A vote is simply an instrument through which you exercise your power. This power doesn't have to be expressed through a physical vote, though it might be. You probably don't realize it, but you exercise your power in several ways already, in addition to voting for your nation's leader.

When you go to your local supermarket to buy a product, say a particular brand of toothpaste, what are you doing in effect? You are voting for that brand. While you haven't actually voted for the product, you have cast your vote through the money you've paid. If you don't like the product, you can always "fire" it and "vote" for a different one next time. Because you have so much power over them, companies are always campaigning (advertising) and falling over themselves to get your "vote" (your money).

In fact, there can be dictators in the economy too. For example, one brand of product can dominate the market, and the company can then do what it feels like once it has the consumers trapped. A large airline can keep dropping its prices such that smaller airlines are unable to compete. Once the smaller airlines die, the large airline can start hiking its prices again. Consumers will have only one airline to choose from and hence will have to put up with shoddy, overpriced, and arrogant service.

Economists even have a term to describe these market dictators: monopolies. Hence, free market economies have mechanisms in place to ensure that companies don't abuse their dominant positions. And note that we call our market economies "free."

Another example of the power equation is the status of women in marriages. Men had all the power in a marriage through religious sanction, economic clout, and sheer physical strength. Unsurprisingly, men were dictators – because once a woman "voted in" her husband through marriage, there was no way out. Although she had the "right to vote," she could vote only once. In the case of forced marriages, she didn't even have that right. In either case, her husband was then dictator-for-life. Either religion didn't sanction divorce, or if it did, there was a social stigma attached to divorce. Moreover, there was no economic or legal support outside marriage. Women had to stay in the marriage whether or not they liked it; quite inevitably, men behaved like dictators.

To combat the abuse of power, women launched a freedom movement. The name of that movement? The Women's Liberation Movement. Women today have greater protection through law, are able to work to provide for themselves, there's far less importance placed on religious sanction, and the stigma of divorce has all but disappeared. It's not surprising that many women now "vote out" their husbands through divorce.

Returning to the workplace, strange though it may sound, your boss already has the right to vote – and you're the candidate. How? When your boss evaluates your performance through an appraisal process, he or she is effectively voting for you to stay on or not. If you get a rating of "satisfactory" or higher, you're voted in, and if you're rated "unsatisfactory," you're voted out.

Viewed from the standpoint of power, the idea of voting isn't bizarre. Now, just like your boss can vote for you, how can you vote for your boss? To answer that, we need to look at how power is wielded by a boss. The main instrument through which a boss's power is expressed is the appraisal. So the subordinate must have equal powers – the power to appraise the boss. An overall rating of satisfactory to outstanding would qualify as a vote in favor of the boss, and a low rating would qualify as a vote against.

Are subordinates' pay packets affected by the rating their bosses give them? Then the bosses' pay packets should be affected by the rating their subordinates give them. If the bottom 10 percent of all employees are fired, the bottom 10 percent of all bosses (as rated by their subordinates) should be fired. The objective is to not get rid of the power that bosses have. It's to balance the power. It's to get them to use that power responsibly and fairly. Having said all this, ideally, the subordinates would actually be able to cast votes to make the process explicit. The boss would be a true leader then.

Yes, organizations do try to provide a semblance of power balance through tools such as 360-degree feedback. But that's like a dictator asking for feedback because you don't have the power to fire him. Worse, it puts the subordinates in a rather tricky position because although they are told to give honest feedback, their hands are tied. This means that subordinates dress up their bosses' weaknesses as strengths – for example, "My boss is too driven." That might be a polite way to say, "He's an abusive slave driver who expects me to work 24 hours a day." But to the boss, that would come across as a compliment.

So the 360-degree review doesn't give us honest answers. And even if bosses say they want honest feedback, there's no way you can tell how they'll react when they actually get that feedback. It would take an incredibly brave subordinate, and an incredibly mature boss, to do the 360-degree review process right. As we know only too well, it's incredibly hard to find these incredible people.

Yet, all this talk of voting and balancing power may appear foolishly idealistic. It even sounds crazy, but is it as crazy as it sounds?

## What madness is this?

To an all-powerful dictator looking in from the outside, a free system appears weak and vulnerable. After all, citizens openly criticize their leaders. The leaders squabble with one another. People who back different leaders squabble with one another. Issues are openly debated. The media ridicules leaders on the front page of newspapers and on primetime TV. People lambaste their leaders online. If citizens don't like their leaders, they throw them out. How messy is that, compared with a neat, tightly controlled, command-and-control system?

Even so, we know that dictatorship systems produce poor results. Countries with elected leaders aren't unorganized anarchies. Despite their chaotic appearance, free systems are tremendously powerful. So we know this for sure: success comes from freedom, and hence, employees must have the right to vote for their bosses.

Say the space shuttles' Boisjoly or Rocha and their engineers had the power to substantially cut their managers' pay, or even fire (vote out) their bosses. Don't you think perhaps their bosses would have listened more carefully? Would Enron, WorldCom, or Tyco have happened, if the whistleblowers had power over their bosses?

As an aside, large companies say they want to foster an entrepreneurial culture. They want to be like small companies which can be nimble by virtue of their size. But if it was just a question of size, why are free, large countries (such as the United States) far more entrepreneurial than small countries run by dictators? Because the question is not big versus small, but freedom versus fear.

As we progress further into the 21st century, the pace of change is manic. A hierarchical organization will never be able to cope with this pace and is headed for extinction. Hence, we need to move from a hierarchical worldview to a paradigm in which the organization is a collection of relationships between free people. To capture this new worldview, I propose a new kind of organization chart (see opposite).

You will notice there's no hierarchy. Yet, the relationships between individuals are still captured – the arrows tell us who a person's leader is. The arrows here do not represent a power relationship. There's no rigid top-down structure to the chart – you can put any person anywhere in the chart, and draw the rest of the organization around that person.

Even if you agree with everything you've read so far, you still probably have several concerns. Let's address a few major "buts:"

- But what about the politics?
- But won't this turn into a popularity contest?
- But how do you ensure workplace justice?

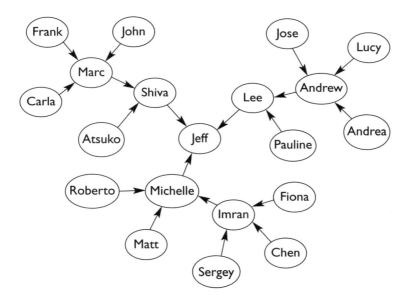

# 21

# BUT …

## What about the politics?

Won't there be politics? Most definitely there will be politics. However, what is politics but a complex interplay of human relationships? And it's not like dictatorial systems don't suffer from politics. They do. In fact, the politics in dictatorial systems can be particularly brutal: if you get it wrong, you die. At the workplace, you're well aware of the politics that goes on. The politics may be understated, but it's there and you know it's there. Under a free system, the politics will not go away.

The only difference is that the nature of politics will change. It's going to be the politics of freedom, not the politics of fear. It's just a question of choosing the lesser of the two evils. Which kind of politics would you prefer? You could think, "I hate politics, whether it's the politics of a fear system or a free system." But the reality is that as long as human beings interact, there is going to be politics.

Our free-system politicians live with the thought that they are going to gain or lose votes all the time. It's a state of being. Workplace leaders will have to cultivate the same mindset that our politicians live with daily. They will need to become comfortable with being ridiculed or criticized all the time. They will need to be comfortable with seeing cartoons of themselves being splashed across the company newspaper or intranet. And most of all, they will have to start worrying about what their subordinates are thinking of them.

## Won't this result in a popularity contest?

If everyone gets to vote for their boss, you're probably worried that this could turn into a popularity contest; the best person for the job isn't elected. But again, think about it. We're talking adults here, even though you might doubt the intelligence of adults. When you vote for the leader of your country, do you vote for the person you like, or do you vote for the person who, in your opinion, is going to be the most effective leader?

Let's take another example. Say you're taking some classes, and you're allowed to vote for a specific teacher. Would you choose the teacher who will go easy on you, a teacher who's willing to give you simple tests and good grades, or a teacher who is great at teaching, and is not willing to bend the rules so it looks like you're succeeding on the tests?

There's simply no doubt that you will choose the person who's most effective at teaching you. You know that an easy and forgiving boss may do what's good for you, but if it hurts the interests of the company, the company could go bust, which only hurts your interests.

Assume we've got the "popularity contest" problem nailed. But if both the boss and subordinate get to appraise each other, what happens if there's a stalemate between a boss and a subordinate? Who decides who's right and who's wrong? We will need to introduce the concept of workplace justice.

## Ensuring workplace justice

Will we need to bring in lawyers and the entire judicial system into our offices? Well, yes and no. Yes, because in some cases, you do need someone impartial to arbitrate on issues. No, because you don't need to replicate the entire judicial system. In some ways, just the fact that you have a system of justice at the workplace will ensure that people try to play fair.

Currently, the concept of fairness and justice doesn't even exist – or if it does, it's down to an individual's conscience. Unless there's gross abuse which is illegal, the folks in human resources (HR) don't need to get involved with boss issues, and mostly they don't. Most of us labor under the misconception that HR's job is to help employees, especially help them get justice.

As Sally Bibb says in *The Stone Age Company*:

> It is a commonly held fallacy that if you have a problem with your boss you can go to HR and they will help. Most HR people have no interest in getting involved with these tricky issues for which there are no clear-cut rules. ... Most focus on policy and policing, and the majority haven't got the courage to stand up to badly behaved bosses.[152]

Why is this? It's partly because HR's job is rarely defined in terms of helping employees. If anything, HR's job by default becomes serving the ruling administration. The problem is that HR people make nice, people-friendly noises as they are meant to, and you naively think, "They will help me." But in reality, their job isn't to help you with your boss issues. This is no indictment of HR, only an acceptance of the reality that they work under.

In the absence of HR doing anything meaningful in terms of ensuring fairness, and the lack of formal mechanisms to specifically address boss–subordinate issues, there's no institutional justice. And however much we may hate the concept of an institution, we need to realize that we're already working for institutions. If we're already in an institution, it makes sense to have justice embedded in the institution – there's nothing worse than an institution without fairness. As we know only too well, such institutions and bosses can quickly turn into Frankenstein's monsters if we're not careful.

While we don't have to create a judicial system, what we can have is someone of the nature of an ombudsman to serve as an independent, but internal, functionary. Essentially, an ombudsman is someone with the authority to investigate complaints between an institution and its employees, or students and a university, and so on. Although ombudsmen serve a variety of needs and functions, we need to assign one to work exclusively for boss–subordinate relationships and conflicts. The ombudsman is outside the formal chain of command, and as such, doesn't need to toe the bosses' line. The idea is that there's a neutral person to resolve disputes. This will send out the signal that boss–subordinate relationships are taken seriously.

Workplace justice is not a new phenomenon or idea. Currently, one body that exists to address workplace injustice is the workers' union. But there are several problems with unions as a mechanism to seek justice.

First, unions typically address issues that affect a large number of employees – pay, working conditions, and so on. Unions are more inclined to worry about legal rights of workers in general, rather than a non-legal problem you may have with your boss.

We know that not all boss-related problems are uniform or legal in nature. Most bosses are aware of what's legal and what's not, and tend to stay within those limits. But as we know, there are many things a boss can do to make your life a living hell while still staying well within legal boundaries. Subordinates may have little evidence or perhaps none at all.

Second, unions are seen by management as a headache and best avoided. Third, the union might be too big a hammer with which to hit the relatively "small" nail that happens to be your individual matter with your boss. While the "small" nail is to you a huge matter, it may not make sense for the union to intervene on your behalf. So unless you are affected by the same issues as everybody else, this leaves you pretty much alone and powerless.

In any case, most employees prefer to have things sorted out internally before taking legal steps. People do realize that not only is it time-consuming and expensive to sue, it's also counterproductive, particularly if they want to continue working in the same organization.

It goes without saying that the ombudsman should guarantee privacy, confidentiality, and most important of all, freedom from reprisals. Over time, an organization will get better at resolving these issues. Like our judicial systems, they will develop a history of cases that they can draw upon. Once these cases are resolved, they can be made public to the internal organization so that employees can learn about what works and what doesn't.

Now, if you are a CEO or a top dog in your organization, where do you go from here?

# 22

# A CALL TO ARMS:
# A SPECIAL NOTE
# TO CEOs AND
# OTHER TOP
# MANAGERS

The message is simple really: change before something bad happens. If you're looking for even more reasons to change in addition to everything you've read so far, the benefits of the new system will be felt in five areas that are key to you:

- identifying real leaders
- accountability
- teamwork
- instilling a sense of ownership in employees
- productivity.

## Identifying real leaders

One of your major jobs is to identify future leaders in your company. If subordinates vote for their leaders, your decision is made. It becomes very easy to see who's consistently getting the votes. It has to be said that this is a double-edged sword, though. On one hand, it makes your life a lot easier. On the other hand, it takes power away from you – you can no longer be the lord and master, bestowing leadership "gifts" on other people.

## Accountability

What is the non-negotiable trait of true leaders? Accountability to their people. Are bosses accountable to their subordinates? No. But just like leaders of countries, bosses will become accountable to subordinates if they have to be voted in. This is fairly obvious.

What's less obvious is that subordinates will have to become more accountable too. Currently, subordinates are accountable to their bosses. While that sounds like accountability enough, it's not true accountability because subordinates have a couple of great get-out clauses if things go wrong: "I was just obeying orders" or "I wasn't told to do anything."

In most cases, inaction is better than action. You can't be held accountable for doing nothing or going with the boss's flow, whereas if you do something against your boss's wishes, you could get into trouble.

Recall the disaster in Tenerife. If the flight engineer had brought the KLM plane to a halt against his captain's command, hundreds of people could still be alive. He didn't do that almost certainly because he didn't want to countermand his boss. And it's acceptable to not countermand your boss. On the other hand, if the flight engineer knew he would be held to account if he didn't stop the plane, wouldn't he have stopped it?

If subordinates are allowed to vote for their leaders, it puts more responsibility on the subordinates themselves. They will not be able to say, "I didn't have the power to overrule my boss." As a boss, this should only please you. Carrying all the burden of responsibility on your shoulders is a very heavy burden to carry indeed.

## Teamwork

If teamwork could be bottled up and sold, the company selling it would make billions. If a "team player" medicine could be sold as tablets, everyone would buy it.

What's a team? The standard definition goes something like this: people working together for a common cause and pulling in the same direction. But remember that in groupthink, everybody's working for a common cause and pulling in the same direction – and that looks a lot like teamwork. The only problem is that everyone's going in the direction the boss wants them to go. Team members don't necessarily feel involved.

In contrast, the fundamental attribute of real teamwork is that everybody feels involved, and everyone is entitled to have an independent viewpoint. If you're going with the boss's flow, that's not involvement. That's sailing with the current. The first step in making everyone feel genuinely involved is getting them to vote for their leader. It makes subordinates more willing to contribute, and makes them more willing to either take the credit or the flak, depending on the outcome.

## Instilling a sense of ownership in employees

A common way that you motivate employees is to grant them stock options. The idea is that since employees have an equity stake in the company, they will feel like company owners and work accordingly. This has its benefits of course.

There's one major flaw with this logic though. What's the use telling subordinates "You are a part-owner of this company," when at the same time they know they can be fired by their bosses? You're sending mixed signals – you're dangling a carrot and the boss is wielding a stick. When you mix the "You can get rich" signal with the "Your boss can fire you" signal, the equity stake gets diluted.

The other problem with the stock options "carrot" is that it can work in reverse: In a bid to retain their stock options, subordinates can behave even more submissively because they have more to lose. Why antagonize the boss when a year down the line, the options are going to vest and the new big home and five-star holiday is going to become a reality? Better to blindly obey the boss than put the family dream at risk.

## Productivity

One of the things that you almost certainly obsess about is employee productivity, because it has a direct impact on your numbers. But it's one thing to make employees productive by making your company processes more efficient or training employees to work better. It's another thing altogether to make employees more productive by giving them more freedom.

There's a fascinating experiment in which subjects were asked to solve some complex puzzles. The subjects were divided into two groups, and random noise was played in the background. One group's members were provided with a switch with which they could turn off the noise, while the other group was not given the switch. The results were stunning. The group with the switch solved five times more puzzles than the switchless group. Amazingly, the subjects with the switch didn't even use it.[153]

So the mere knowledge that they had some control over their environment made them more productive. Recall the Whitehall study that showed just how important job control is. Imagine the difference in productivity it would make if subordinates had power over their leaders.

## What do you do now?

Let me take you back to the story of the emperor's new clothes. Whenever the story is proffered as an illustration of people being intentionally deluded, the story always ends with the revelation that the emperor wasn't wearing any clothes. But that's not where the story ends.

The most telling part of the story is what the emperor did after the child shouted out that their ruler was naked. What did the emperor do? He proceeded on his way acting as though he really was wearing clothes. He did this because he had to keep up the pretence that unlike everyone around him, he wasn't stupid – that he was the most intelligent person in his kingdom and therefore fit to continue ruling.

If you agree with this book and don't do anything about it, you'll be like the emperor – pretending that nothing has happened. Of course, changing the system isn't easy. But you've got to make a start, and the first thing you can do is to publicly declare that the existing system needs to be replaced with a free system. This declaration is critically important, because all your future actions will stem from this.

You don't need to know the way ahead. You don't need to have all the answers up front. If there's conviction, the inevitable obstacles and practicalities can be worked out. If you think it's not practical, just be glad that the founding fathers and mothers of our nations didn't think the same way. If they had waited until they had all the answers, we'd still be living in fear systems. They had nobody to guide them and yet they embarked on an awesome and magnificent journey, the fruits of which we live with daily. We now have countries that have forged institutional frameworks and undertake massive logistical exercises to ensure that hundreds of millions of people can choose their leaders. How impractical is that?

Here are a few more things you can do to get started right away:

- Redraw your organization chart according to the new one. Do away with giving grades to job positions. You can continue giving grand job titles, though.
- Start a performance appraisal process in which subordinates evaluate their leader's performance. Factor in these ratings to the leader's compensation package. You can start small – a small team or section.
- Encourage employees to start writing critical articles or draw cartoons of their bosses, and publish these on the company intranet or in-house magazine. It will be difficult at first for the bosses, but like our political leaders, they will soon accept it as part of the game.
- Unless they're voted in, stop calling managers or supervisors "leaders." They're not leaders and by calling them leaders, you're misleading yourself and everyone else.

You may still be bewildered, angered, or think all this is pure insanity. But that only puts you in a better position to understand the plight of contemporary dictators, who are completely flummoxed when they're continually admonished by our country's leaders for not allowing their subjects to vote. To someone who's never experienced a free system, the idea of voting for your leader is totally alien, dangerous, and foolhardy.

If you're a business owner or entrepreneur, you probably think it's crazy to let someone "vote you out" of power. After all, it's your business, something you've created yourself through risk taking and hard work. How can an employee fire you?

Obviously, no one can fire you. But if you were "voted out," you would hire a manager who was better at managing people. You must not confuse leadership with ownership. In fact, many founders are fired by investors if it's felt that the founders cannot manage the transition of growing a small company to a bigger one. So the idea of firing yourself isn't a novel one: you still make your money. You may lose control, but if it means your business not only survives but thrives, wouldn't that be a lot better?

Will this new system be perfect? No. Countries in which people vote for their leaders aren't perfect either, but they're a lot better than the alternative. And remember that even if you decide to continue with a dictatorship system, you'll soon come up against a competitor with a free system.

If as always you're looking for evidence of a company with a free system, go no farther than Semco, a Brazilian company. Its around 3,000 employees have a say in virtually everything – from the way the cafeteria runs, to the company strategy, to working hours and to of course, the boss. Ricardo Semler, Semco's owner, wrote a book called *Maverick* about his experiments and experiences.[154] The company is very successful in a country that has been battered by both political and economic storms.

## A short note to bosses

First off, if you think of yourself as a good boss, do something to prove it: ask your team for a show of hands to see if they'd vote you in as boss. If they're unwilling to do a show of hands, you have your answer. Alternatively, you could have an anonymous vote. Obviously, you've got to be mature about it – if you don't like what you get, don't take it out on your subordinates. If you like what you get, you should be the first one to welcome the move to a free system, because you will finally get the recognition you deserve. You fought against the programming of the system and won. It's no mean feat.

As a boss, you probably worry about your subordinates resenting you. But it's not necessarily your fault. You may ask your subordinates for a favor, but to them, that's a direct order. Once there's a free system, a favor will stay a favor. It won't breed resentment. As you know only too well, no one likes being under the control of somebody else. If you're under someone else's control, you're going to sometimes take offence when none was intended.

What if you own the company and you obviously cannot be voted out? You'd need to make a distinction between a subordinate working in your interests directly, and a subordinate working for the interests of your organization. So if you're the owner's personal assistant, she would obviously be your "customer." But before she hired you, she would need to make it clear that she will be your dictator. That way, there would be no surprises and no false expectations of leadership behavior.

Most importantly, the fact that the "system" influences your behavior is no excuse to cast aside all notions of personal responsibility.

## A short note for abused subordinates

You're probably going through hell. It's said that the only meaningful words of comfort that you can offer a person who is close to death is this: You are not alone. Feeling alone and isolated is perhaps the worst fate that can befall a human being.

As someone working for an abusive boss, you probably feel intensely alone and isolated. It's the nature of the system to induce those feelings. But remember this: you are not alone, millions share your plight.

We just need to get everyone talking about the issue and this book is just one way of doing that. Hopefully, this discussion will soon burst out into the open, and our workplace systems will change for the better.

## And finally ...

As we come to the end of book, I'll finish off with a little "thought experiment" for you. It involves a bit of time travel, so that's why it's only a thought experiment.

# Section

## V

# Conclusion:
# A Thought
# Experiment

# 23

# BEFORE YOU GO,
# A LITTLE TEST

Say I am the king of a mid-sized kingdom a few centuries ago. Although I'm not in the middle of a war or any major crisis right now, I have several serious problems:

- My hostile neighboring king has developed some new weapons, with which he intends to wipe us out.
- My weapons factory is turning out faulty, primitive, and low-quality weapons.
- My other "good" neighbor, with whom I barter several essential grains, is considering joining my competitor, potentially starving us.
- There are spies in my own kingdom and I don't know what information they are passing on to my enemies.
- My people tend to be ill and life expectancy is low.

Having said all this, I have several things going for me:

- I seem to be well loved, going by the number of my portraits that my subjects have put up all over the kingdom.
- I am highly educated and intelligent by the standards of my era.
- I have some extremely talented and loyal friends, who I can really count on.

■ My wife – the queen – is very attractive, and my powerful but hostile neighbour is in love with her; that's the only reason he hasn't attacked me so far. On the other hand, it also gives him a very good reason to attack. But my queen is standing by me and tells me she will never run off with the enemy king.

Now that you are aware of my problems, I want some advice. My aim is to be the richest and most powerful king so I don't have these worries in future. I want someone who can think differently – I've tried many advisors but they haven't helped.

But I also have a secret trump card, a little magic lamp that bestows on me an incredible power: I am allowed to bring in anyone from the 21st century to advise me about what to do. And I am calling you. You will be my advisor.

You are not allowed to bring anything: no computers, no newspapers, no high-tech weapons, no aircraft designs, no magazines, no books, or reference information of any sort. You cannot make any calls to anybody (we don't have phones). You are only allowed to bring your knowledge and wisdom.

Not only am I calling you for advice, I am giving you another big thing: my crown. You will be the absolute and supreme ruler of my subjects for a year, so you can be sure they will obey you.

Knowing everything that you do know, what would you do to help me? Please spend some time thinking over the problems and suggest some solutions, in order of priority. At the very least, come up with the first thing you would do. Don't read ahead.

(Page intentionally left blank; you can write some of your answers here.)

## What's your answer?

Well, knowing what you do, here's what I hope you would do: Give up the throne the king has given to you. Then declare that people will vote for their leaders. Implementation will take time, energy, and effort. But you would start out by making a declaration that you intend to create a free system in which people choose their own leaders.

You already know that free systems are the best way to produce strong, healthy, wealthy, and powerful countries. If you didn't give this answer, why not?

You're probably thinking this is impossible. This can't happen in reality. That's why it's only a thought experiment, right? Which kingdom's monarch would willingly give up power, step aside, and let elected commoners lead? Not only is it impossible to conceptualize, it's impractical. How do you go about creating a process in which millions of commoners vote for their kingdom's leader, something that's never been attempted before? It would be madness.

But madly enough, there is a kingdom in the real world in which this has happened. Even more madly, this kingdom still exists without being over-run by commoner anarchists. And it's not some dot of a kingdom in a remote part of the planet. This kingdom is called the United Kingdom of Great Britain and Northern Ireland. The queen is the head of that country, and she still retains her pomp and splendor. She's called Her Majesty and people still bow or curtsy to her. The government is called Her Majesty's Government. The air force is called the Royal Air Force. The navy is called the Royal Navy. Yet, despite all the royalty, elected commoners run the show.

It gets weirder. While the Royal family retains its eminent position in public life, members of the family are often openly ridiculed. People make jokes about them and laugh at them. They're lampooned by the media. Their every move is watched – not only by their security staff, but also by opportunistic photographers.

Looking at it this way, it boggles the mind to see what's happened there, doesn't it? Insane? Yes. Fanciful? Yes. Impractical? No. Free? Yes. Stable? Yes. Strong? Yes. Wealthy? Yes.

This thought experiment shows you just how ingrained the "dictator" mindset can be. If someone gives you power, you're very likely to accept it without a second thought. You're not going to question it. You're going to take that power and start working out answers to problems. You're not going to look at the bigger issue of making systemic changes.

Why do we take and use power so easily? We do this because when someone tells us that "you're a leader" we feel good, if not great, and proceed to take that power quite happily. We assume that the authority we have over the subjects is legitimate. And there lies our downfall.

Still, it wouldn't be so bad if we were only dragging ourselves down. The bigger tragedy is that we're taking our kids down with us, because the influence of our workplace dictatorship systems does not stop at the workplace. Have you ever wondered why our schools and other education institutions value and inculcate conformity? To a large extent, it's because they're preparing kids to work in dictatorship systems.

We've come to the end of this book. If you've got this far, I would like to thank you for taking the time to read it. At the very least, I hope I've got you thinking. And if there's only one thing I'd like you to take away from this book, it's this: *If you aren't elected, you're a dictator.*

# NOTES

1     General Tommy Franks, *American Soldier*, HarperCollins (2005), p133.
2     Jack Welch, *Winning*, HarperCollins (2005), p309.
3     Sally Bibb, *The Stone Age Company*, Marshall Cavendish Business and Cyan (2005), p72.
4     Frederick Winslow Taylor, *The Principles of Scientific Management* (1911) http://melbecon.unimelb.edu.au/het/taylor/sciman.htm# Ch2.
5     Stanford Prison Experiment, A simulation study of the psychology of imprisonment conducted at Stanford University, http://www.prisonexp.org.
6     Stanford Prison Experiment, Still powerful after all these years, http://www.stanford.edu/dept/news/pr/97/970108prisonexp.html.
7     Stanford Prison Experiment, Parole board, http://www.prisonexp.org/slide-32.htm.
8     MSNBC, Maj. Gen. Antonio M. Taguba, "US Army report on Iraqi prisoner abuse," May 4, 2004, http://www.msnbc.msn.com/id/4894001; BBC News, "Iraqi abuse photos spark outrage," April 30, 2004, http://news.bbc.co.uk/2/hi/middle_east/3672901.stm.
9     Thomas E. Ricks, *Fiasco: The American Military Adventure in Iraq*, Penguin (2006), p198.
10    "Triple suicide at Guantanamo camp," BBC News, June 11, 2006, http://news.bbc.co.uk/2/hi/americas/5068228.stm.
11    Claudia Dreifus, "Finding Hope in Knowing the Universal Capacity for Evil", *New York Times*, April 3, 2007 , http://www.nytimes.com/2007/04/03/science/03conv.html?em&ex=1175745 600&en=a0bd6e7b4f3465db&ei=5087%0A
12    John Simpson, *Strange Places, Questionable People*, Macmillan (1998), p445.

13  J. M. Darley and C. D. Batson, "From Jerusalem to Jericho: A study of situational and dispositional variables in helping behavior," *Journal of Personality and Social Psychology* (1973) 27: 100–8, http://faculty.babson.edu/krollag/org_site/soc_psych/darley_samarit.html; Gilbert Harman, "Moral philosophy meets social psychology," Princeton University, http://www.princeton.edu/~harman/Papers/Virtue.html.

14  James Q. Wilson and George L. Kelling, "Broken windows," March 1982, http://www.theatlantic.com/ideastour/archive/windows.mhtml.

15  A good description of the broken windows theory and how it was implemented in the New York subway and the city itself can be found in Malcolm Gladwell's *The Tipping Point*, Little, Brown (2000), pp141–6.

16  William Bratton and George Kelling, "There are no cracks in the broken windows," February 28, 2006, http://www.nationalreview.com/comment/bratton_kelling200602281015.asp.

17  Steven D. Levitt and Stephen J. Dubner, *Freakonomics*, Chapter 4: "Where have all the criminals gone?" HarperCollins (2005), pp117–44.

18  Malcolm Gladwell, *The Tipping Point*, Little, Brown (2000), pp133–68.

19  Definition given by the late Austrian biologist Ludwig von Bertalanffy, http://www.systems-thinking.org/systems/systems.htm.

20  A good discussion on systems thinking can be found in Peter M. Senge's book, *The Fifth Discipline*, Random House (1990).

21  Horst W. J. Rittel and Melvin M. Weber, *Dilemmas in a General Theory of Planning*, Elsevier Scientific (1973), pp155–69, http://www.uctc.net/mwebber/Rittel+Webber+Dilemmas+General_Theory_of_Planning.pdf.

22  Greater London Authority press release, June 6, 2003, http://www.london.gov.uk/view_press_release.jsp?releaseid=1770.

23  Interview: Archbishop Desmond Tutu, interviewed by John Carlin, http://www.pbs.org/wgbh/pages/frontline/shows/mandela/interviews/tutu.html.

24  Columbia Accident Investigation Board, Report Volume 1, p130, http://caib.nasa.gov/news/report/pdf/vol1/full/caib_report_volume1.pdf.
Diane Vaughan has written a book in which she analyzes the *Challenger* space shuttle disaster through the lens of the "normalization of deviance." *The Challenger Launch Decision: Risky Technology, Culture, and Deviance at NASA*, University of Chicago Press (1996).

25    "Do I dare say something?" Q&A with Amy Edmondson, Harvard Business School Working Knowledge, March 20, 2006, http://hbswk.hbs.edu/item/5261.html.

26    University of Plymouth, 'Depression and learned helplessness,' http://salmon.psy.plym.ac.uk/year2/psy221depression/psy221dep ression.htm.

27    Sally Bibb, *The Stone Age Company*, Cyan (2005), p59.

28    Benedict Carey, "Fear in the workplace: the bullying boss," *New York Times*, June 22, 2004, http://query.nytimes.com/gst/ fullpage.html?sec=health&res=9E04E7DE1339F931A15755C0 A9629C8B63.

29    Jack Welch, *Winning*, HarperCollins (2005), p303.

30    Biography: Idi Amin Dada, http://africanhistory.about.com/od/ biography/a/bio_amin.htm.

31    BBC country profile: North Korea, http://news.bbc.co.uk/2/hi/ asia-pacific/country_profiles/1131421.stm.

32    Dr Jane E. Ferrie (ed.), Dr Ruth Bell et al., *Work, Stress and Health: The Whitehall II Study* (2004) p4, http://www.ucl.ac.uk/ whitehallII/research/Whitehallbooklet.pdf.
      Hans Bosma, Michael G. Marmot, Harry Hemingway, Amanda C. Nicholson, Eric Brunner, and Stephen A. Stansfeld, "Low job control and risk of coronary heart disease in Whitehall II (prospective cohort) study," *British Medical Journal* (1997), http://www.bmj.com/cgi/content/full/314/7080/558.

33    Ferrie, Bell, et al. (2004), p6.

34    Ibid, pp3–4.

35    Ibid, p4.

36    Sir Michael Marmot interview: Conversations with history, Institute of International Studies, UC Berkeley (2002), http://globe trotter.berkeley.edu/people2/Marmot/marmot-con3.html.

37    Ferrie, Bell, et al. (2004), p4.

38    Bosma et al. (1997).

39    Ibid.

40    Ferrie, Bell, et al. (2004), p6.

41    Álvaro Franco, Carlos Álvarez-Dardet, and Maria Teresa Ruiz, "Effect of democracy on health: ecological study," *British Medical Journal*, http://www.bmj.com/cgi/content/full/329/ 7480/1421.

42    N. Wager, G. Fieldman and T. Hussey, '"The effect on ambulatory blood pressure of working under favourably and unfavourably perceived supervisors," *British Medical Journal* (2003), http://oem.bmj.com/cgi/content/abstract/60/7/468.

43    Secretary of aviation report on Tenerife crash (1978)

http://www.panamair.org/accidents/victor.htm. Other sites refer-
enced include: http://www.tenerifecrash.com and http://www.
airmanshiponline.com/fall99/articoli/05a99-tenerife.htm.

44 Gerard M. Bruggink, "Remembering Tenerife," *Air Line Pilot*
(2000), http://www.airmanshiponline.com/marzo2003/10-Tenerife
%20by%20Bruggink.pdf, p6.

45 Public Broadcasting Service (PBS), "The deadliest plane crash,"
October 17, 2006, http://www.pbs.org/wgbh/nova/transcripts/
3315_planecra.html.

46 Robert L. Helmreich, Ashleigh C. Merritt, and John A. Wilhelm, *The
Evolution of Crew Resource Management Training in Commercial
Aviation*, University of Texas at Austin, http://homepage.
psy.utexas.edu/HomePage/Group/HelmreichLAB/Publications/
pubfiles/Pub235.pdf.

47 Ibid.

48 Mark Hayhurst, "I knew what was about to happen," *Guardian*,
January 23, 2001, http://www.guardian.co.uk/g2/story/0,3604,
426586,00.html.

49 James Oberg, "Deadly space lessons go unheeded," MSNBC,
January 26, 2005, http://www.msnbc.msn.com/id/6872105/
page/2.

50 Morton Thiokol is now a part of Alliant Techsystems Inc.,
http://www.atk.com.

51 Report of the Presidential Commission on the Space Shuttle
*Challenger* accident (1986), Vol 4, p1406, http://history.nasa.gov/
rogersrep/v4part7.htm#4.

52 National Public Radio (NPR), "*Challenger*: reporting a disaster's
cold, hard facts," January 28, 2006, http://www.npr.org/
templates/story/story.php?storyId=5175151.

53 Report of the Presidential Commission on the Space Shuttle *Challenger* accident (1986), Vol 4, p1420, http://history.nasa.gov/
rogersrep/v4part7.htm#4.

54 "Engineering ethics: the Space Shuttle *Challenger* disaster,"
Department of Philosophy and Department of Mechanical Engineering, Texas A&M University, http://ethics.tamu.edu/ethics/
shuttle/shuttle1.htm.

55 Joe Trento, "*Challenger*: twenty years later, lessons never
learned," January 26, 2006, http://www.storiesthatmatter.org/
index.php?option=com_content&task=view&id=17&
Itemid=40.

56 Report of the Presidential Commission on the Space Shuttle *Challenger* accident, Chapter 5: "The contributing cause of the accident" (1986), http://science.ksc.nasa.gov/shuttle/missions/51-l/
docs/rogers-commission/Chapter-5.txt.

57  Ibid.

58  Report of the Presidential Commission on the Space Shuttle
    *Challenger* accident, (1986), Vol 5, p1622, http://history.nasa.gov/
    rogersrep/ v5part1a.htm#2.

59  Report of the Presidential Commission on the Space Shuttle
    *Challenger* accident, (1986), Vol 4, p1383, http://history.nasa.
    gov/rogersrep/v4part7.htm#4.

60  Ibid, p1385.

61  Report of the Presidential Commission on the Space Shuttle
    *Challenger* accident, (1986), Vol 4, p1456, http://history.nasa.
    gov/rogersrep/v4part7.htm#5.

62  Roger M Boisjoly, "Ethical decisions: Morton Thiokol and the
    space shuttle *Challenger* disaster," Online Ethics Center for Engi-
    neering and Science at Case Western Reserve University (2005),
    http://www.onlineethics.com/essays/shuttle/telecon.html.

63  Report of the Presidential Commission on the Space Shuttle
    *Challenger* accident (1986) Vol 4, pp1419–20, http://history.nasa.
    gov/rogersrep/v4part7.htm#4.

64  Report of the Presidential Commission on the Space Shuttle
    *Challenger* accident, (1986) Vol 4, pp1487, http://history.nasa.
    gov/rogersrep/v4part7.htm#5.

65  Ibid, p1488.

66  Roger M. Boisjoly, "Ethical decisions: Morton Thiokol and the
    space shuttle *Challenger* disaster," Online Ethics Center for Engi-
    neering and Science at Case Western Reserve University (2005),
    http://www.onlineethics.com/moral/boisjoly/RB1–6.html.

67  Report of the Presidential Commission on the Space Shuttle
    *Challenger* accident, (1986), Organization chart, Morton
    Thiokol, January 27, 1986, Meeting participants, http://history.
    nasa.gov/rogersrep/v1p231.htm.

68  Report of the Presidential Commission on the Space Shuttle
    *Challenger* accident, (1986), Vol 4, p1421, http://history.nasa.
    gov/rogersrep/v4part7.htm#4.

69  Ibid, pp1451–2.

70  Joe Trento, "*Challenger*: twenty years later, lessons never
    learned," January 26, 2006, http://www.storiesthatmatter.org/
    index.php?option=com_content&task=view&id=17&Itemid=40.

71  Heesun Wee, "The right way to blow the whistle," *BusinessWeek
    Online*, January 30, 2002, http://www.businessweek.com/
    bwdaily/dnflash/jan2002/nf20020130_7564.htm.

72  Elizabeth Kane, "Is PE license a boon to ethics in industry?,"
    National Society of Professional Engineers (1997), http://
    www.asa3.org/archive/asa/199703/0200.html.

73 James Surowiecki, *The Wisdom of Crowds*, Abacus (2005), p254.
74 R. P. Feynman, "Appendix F: Personal observations on the reliability of the Shuttle," http://science.ksc.nasa.gov/shuttle/missions/51-l/docs/rogers-commission/Appendix-F.txt.
75 Philip M. Boffey, "Suits against maker of space rocket thrown out," *New York Times*, September 3, 1988, http://query.nytimes.com/gst/fullpage.html?sec=travel&res=940DE6DF 113BF930A3575AC0A96E948260&n=Top%2fNews%2fScienc e%2fTopics%2fSpace%20Shuttle.
76 Andrew J. Dunar and Stephen P. Waring, *Power To Explore: History of Marshall Space Flight Center 1960–1990*, Chapter 9, "The *Challenger* accident," p377, http://history.msfc.nasa.gov/book/chptnine.pdf.
77 Ibid.
78 *Columbia* Accident Investigation Board, Report Vol 1 (2003), p60, http://caib.nasa.gov/news/report/pdf/vol1/full/caib_report_volume1.pdf.
79 James Glanz and John Schwartz, "Dogged engineer's effort to assess shuttle damage," *New York Times*, September 26, 2003, http://www.nytimes.com/2003/09/26/national/nationalspecial/26ENGI.html?ei=5007&en=10772541a545b410&ex=1379908 800&adxnnl=1&partner=USERLAND&adxnnlx=1164395736-dhhq7ApWaraSPgWZRdLkbw.
80 *Columbia* Accident Investigation Board, Report Vol 1 (2003), p140, http://caib.nasa.gov/news/report/pdf/vol1/full/caib_report_volume1.pdf.
81 Ibid, p142.
82 NASA Facts, Mission Management Team telecon, http://www.nasa.gov/pdf/47227main_mmt_030121.pdf.
83 *Columbia* Accident Investigation Board, Report Vol 1 (2003), pp151–2, http://caib.nasa.gov/news/report/pdf/vol1/full/caib_report_volume1.pdf.
84 Ibid, p153.
85 Ibid, p156.
86 Ibid, p154.
87 Glanz and Schwartz (2003).
   Chicken Little is a fable about a chicken that believes the sky is falling; it's also a term that's used to indicate a hysterical, mistaken belief that the end of the world is near.
88 *Columbia* Accident Investigation Board, Report Volume 1 (2003), p157, http://caib.nasa.gov/news/report/pdf/vol1/full/caib_report_volume1.pdf.
89 Ibid, p157.

90   Glanz and Schwartz (2003).
91   *Columbia* Accident Investigation Board, Report Vol 1 (2003), p160, http://caib.nasa.gov/news/report/pdf/vol1/full/caib_report_volume1.pdf.
92   Ibid, p160.
93   Ibid, p160.
94   Ibid, p156.
95   Ibid, p192.
96   Ibid, p161.
97   Joel Bach, "Engineer sounded warnings for *Columbia,*" *ABC News*, July 7, 2003, http://abcnews.go.com/Technology/story?id=97600&page=4.
98   Glanz and Schwartz (2003).
99   Ibid.
100  Ibid.
101  *Columbia* Accident Investigation Board, Report Vol 1 (2003), p170, http://caib.nasa.gov/news/report/pdf/vol1/full/caib_report_volume1.pdf.
102  Ibid, p99.
103  Ibid, p110.
104  Ibid, p109.
105  Ibid, p115.
106  Ibid, p116.
107  Ibid, p117.
108  Ibid, p131.
109  Ibid, p132.
110  Ibid, p134.
111  Ibid, p134.
112  Ibid, p139.
113  Ibid, p169.
114  Ibid, p131.
115  Ibid, p170.
116  Ibid, p172.
117  Ibid, p121.
118  Ibid, p169.
119  Ibid, p99.
120  Ibid, p192.
121  Ibid, p170.
122  Glanz and Schwartz (2003).
123  Report on the US Intelligence Community's Prewar Intelligence Assessments on Iraq (2004), Introduction, p8, http://www.gpo access.gov/serialset/creports/iraq.html.
124  Ibid, p14–24.

125 NBC News, "Meet the press," May 16, 2004, http:// www.msnbc.msn.com/id/4992558.

126 Letter to President Clinton on Iraq, Project for the New American Century, January 26, 1998, http://www.newamericancentury.org/ iraqclintonletter.htm

127 Report on the US Intelligence Community's Prewar Intelligence Assessments on Iraq (2004), Introduction, p16, http:// www.gpoaccess.gov/serialset/creports/iraq.html.

128 Ibid, p19.

129 Thomas E. Ricks, *Fiasco: The American Military Adventure in Iraq*, Penguin (2006), p55.

130 Report on the US Intelligence Community's Prewar Intelligence Assessments on Iraq (2004), Introduction, p13, http:// www.gpoaccess.gov/serialset/creports/iraq.html.

131 Suzanne Goldenberg, "Ex-CIA chief eats humble pie," *Guardian*, April 29, 2005, http://www.guardian.co.uk/usa/story/0,12271, 1472825,00.html.

132 The White House, "President presents Medal of Freedom," December 14, 2004, http://www.whitehouse.gov/news/releases/ 2004/12/20041214-3.html.

133 Thomas E. Ricks (2006), p33.

134 Bob Woodward, *State of Denial*, Simon and Schuster (2006), p219.

135 Ibid, p224.

136 Ibid, p226.

137 Ibid.

138 Michael R. Gordon and General Bernard E. Trainor, *Cobra II: The Inside Story of the Invasion and Occupation of Iraq*, Pantheon (2006), p59.

139 Comprehensive Report of the Special Advisor to the DCI (Director of Central Intelligence) on Iraq's WMD (2004), https://www. cia.gov/cia/reports/iraq_wmd_2004/chap1.html#sect4

140 Ibid.

141 Ibid.

142 Ibid.

143 The White House, Press Conference by the President, November 8, 2006, http://www.whitehouse.gov/news/releases/2006/11/ 20061108-2.html.

144 James Surowiecki, *The Wisdom of Crowds*, Abacus (2004), p231.

145 "Millennium Challenge 02," http://www.jfcom.mil/about/ experiments/mc02.htm; Julian Borger, "Wake-up call," *Guardian*, September 6, 2002, http://www.guardian.co.uk/g2/ story/0,3604, 786992,00.html.

146 Malcolm Gladwell, *Blink*, Penguin (2005), p118.
147 Sean D. Naylor, "War games rigged?" *Army Times*, August 16, 2002, http://www.armytimes.com/story.php?f=1-292925-1060102.php.
148 PBS, Interview with Paul Van Riper, July 8, 2004, http://www.pbs.org/wgbh/pages/frontline/shows/pentagon/interviews/vanriper.html.
149 Charles Darwin, *The Origin of Species* (6th edn), Chapter 3: "Struggle For existence", (1872), http://www.literature.org/authors/darwin-charles/the-origin-of-species-6th-edition/chapter-03.html.
150 Charles Darwin, *The Descent of Man*, Chapter 4 (1901), http://www.biologie.uni-hamburg.de/b-online/e36_descent/descent_chap4.html.
151 *Columbia* Accident Investigation Board, Report Vol 1, p101, http://caib.nasa.gov/news/report/pdf/vol1/full/caib_report_volume1.pdf.
152 Sally Bibb, *The Stone Age Company*, Cyan (2005), pp75–6.
153 Tom Peters, *Strategies for Continuous Learning in the Workplace Part IV* (1988), http://www.tompeters.com/col_entries.php?note=005204&year=1988.
154 Ricardo Semler, *Maverick*, Warner Books (1993).

# ABOUT THE AUTHOR

Chetan Dhruve has worked for several organizations including IBM, Cisco Systems and the Department for International Development (DfID, formerly the aid wing of the British Foreign Office). He is also an entrepreneur, and has co-founded a couple of internet startups.

Chetan has an MBA from Cass Business School (London), an MA in international journalism from City University (London), and a BSc in Mathematics, Physics and Electronics from St Joseph's College, Bangalore University.

You can contact Chetan via his website at:
http://www.cvdhruve.com

# THE TRUTH ABOUT BUSINESS

*Why Your Boss is Programmed to be a Dictator* is part of The Truth About Business series, which tackles some of the most pertinent and sensitive topics in business and work today. The series is edited by Sally Bibb.

Other titles in the series are:

*The Stone Age Company*
Why the companies we work for are dying and how they can be saved
Sally Bibb

*Just for the Money?*
What really motivates us at work
Adrian Furnham with Tom Booth

*Mine's Bigger Than Yours*
Understanding and handling egos at work
Susan Debnam

# The Stone Age Company
Why the companies we work for are dying and how they can be saved

Sally Bibb

*Companies need to change: They are outdated and ineffective in the way they are run and they are losing out in the increasingly competitive world of business.*

That's the view of Sally Bibb, author of this thought-provoking and controversial book, which challenges leaders to think about their organizations and how they should be managed.

The Stone Age company is an uninspiring place to work – it is an organization that has practices that don't work anymore. It talks the talk but doesn't walk the walk. It is characterized by hierarchy, controlling management techniques, managerial bad behavior and spin. Is your company like this?

This book is a wake-up call. It will inspire leaders to reinvent the way businesses are run, encouraging them to turn their organization into a different type of company: A company that thrills its customers, is innovative and efficient, is fun and energizing to work for. Using examples of successful organizations including the Innocent Drinks company, WL Gore, Timberland and Southwest Airlines, and her own personal experiences, Bibb shows what innovative companies do and how they do it.

Written in a clear and inspirational way, unlike traditional management books, *The Stone Age Company* is a book that all managers, leaders, employees, and shareholders should buy if they want to succeed in today's fast-changing business world.

ISBN-10 1-904879-43-8
ISBN-13 978-1-904879-43-5
UK £9.99 / USA $18.95 / CAN $25.95

*Just for the Money?*
What really motivates us at work

Adrian Furnham with Tom Booth

*How many people work just for the money? What is your time actually worth? How does your organization handle the trade-off between the good, the cheap and the fast?*

These are some of the questions asked by Adrian Furnham and Tom Booth, the authors of this thought-provoking book. *Just for the Money?* challenges our assumptions about money in the workplace, at home and in our daily lives.

The book is predicated on four fundamental, evidence-based truths: Most people are far from rational with respect to money; our attitudes to beliefs about our spending and saving of money have much to do with our childhood and early education; at work, money is a powerful demotivator, rather than a powerful motivator; and money and well-being are only tangentially related.

Furnham and Booth explore money and motivation at work, money beliefs, money in society, money and religion, the meaning of money, the importance of money, money as a motivator or demotivator, money and emotions, and money and family. *Just for the Money?* even includes useful tips for helping your children to understand about money and teaching them to be sensible with it.

Unlike traditional business guides, this fascinating book is one that you must buy if you are interested in money!

ISBN-10 1-904879-50-0
ISBN-13 978-1-904879-50-3
UK £9.99 / USA $18.95 / CAN $25.95

*Mine's Bigger Than Yours*
Understanding and handling egos at work

Susan Debnam

*Every workplace has one, maybe several. The manager who radiates charm but never seems to achieve anything; the colleague who is always playing power games; the member of staff so intent on climbing the career ladder that they trample on anyone who stands in their way. They have one thing in common: ego.*

The ego isn't inherently bad, but it needs to be kept in check. In her thought-provoking new book, Susan Debnam argues that many organizations have come to rely on people with big personalities, flamboyance and charisma. Yet if their forcefulness isn't balanced by self-awareness and restraint, they can wreck businesses and bring misery to the people around them.

*Mine's Bigger Than Yours* looks at thriving organizations that have chosen a better option. To get the most out of all their people, they consciously foster an ego-free culture. People can admit they don't know the answer without being ridiculed. They are free to make suggestions, to innovate and to excel. Power and glory are shared, not the preserve of the ego-driven few.

Discover whether your office is ego-free or ego-driven by reading this book – and then find out what to do about it.

ISBN-10 1-904879-64-0
ISBN-13 978-1-904879-64-0
UK £8.99 / USA $14.95 / CAN $20.95